OPERATING THE CHILD PROTECTION SYSTEM

A study of child protection practices in English local authorities

JANE GIBBONS   SUE CONROY   CAROLINE BELL

Social Work Development Unit, University of East Anglia

STUDIES IN CHILD PROTECTION

LONDON: HMSO

Applications for reproduction should be made to HMSO Copyright Unit
First published 1995
Second Impression 1995

ISBN 0 11 321785 4

Acknowledgements

We acknowledge the generous help of social work and administrative staff in the eight authorities who took part in the study. Thanks to them, the researchers were able to track down many records that had seemed to be lost. Child protection advisers who formed a bridge between the researchers and the local authority were particularly important.

We thank Dr David Gordon for the statistics summarised in table 8i. Valuable assistance with data collection was given by: Grace Dedman, Dredagh Dodge, and Ann Lewis.

We are particularly grateful to the members of the Advisory Group, who contributed ideas and constructive criticism over the course of the research:

Dr Carolyn Davies, Department of Health (Chair)
Rosemary Arkley, Department of Health
Jean Gabbott, Tower Hamlets Social Services
Alan Jones, Social Services Inspectorate
Dr Michael Little, Dartington Social Research Unit
Dr Susan Shephard, Department of Health
Veronika Simons, Bexley Social Services (1991 only)
Jim Stokoe, Department of Health
Kathleen Taylor, Department of Health

Table of Contents

List of Tables

List of Figures

Introduction

Function of Child Protection Registers

Child protection registers in England came into being as one of three main means of improving inter-agency communication in the handling of 'non-accidental injury' (NAI) to children. In 1974, following the Inquiry into the death of Maria Colwell, the Department of Health and Social Security (DHSS) advised local and health authorities to form Area Review Committees (now Area Child Protection Committees) to oversee local policy and training arrangements; to ensure that case conferences were held following every suspected case; and to set up a "central record of information" (the register) which was "essential to good communication between the many disciplines involved" (DHSS, 1974).

In contrast to the system of mandatory reporting established in the United States, no legal duty to report cases was established in the United Kingdom. However, the government laid down procedures for agencies to follow in its circulars (DHSS, 1976 & 1980). At this stage registers were still seen mainly as tools to aid inter-agency communication, especially in the early identification of cases, and as sources of data for management and research purposes.

However, studies of how the registers were operating gave continuing cause for concern. It was reported that they were not much used by local professionals in many areas – which obviously limited their value in the early identification of cases (BASW, 1978; ADSS, 1981, 1987; DHSSI, 1990). It was further pointed out that the inclusion of 'suspected' cases raised civil liberties and privacy issues, as well as resulting in large registers, difficult and expensive to administer and probably inaccurate (Hallett & Stevenson, 1980; FRG, 1986). Differing criteria for registration in different authorities have been widely noted (Tilley & Burke, 1988; Cann, 1989). 'Covert' reasons for registration (such as procurement of additional resources for particular families), masked by the stated official criteria, have been documented (Corby & Mills, 1986; Jones et al., 1986). It has often been pointed out that bureaucratic procedures associated with registration do not in themselves protect or benefit children (Geach & Szwed, 1983). Corby concluded that registering a child served a variety of covert functions – such as ranking cases by perceived seriousness and so helping to ration resources, and ensuring reviews of individual social work practice – but felt that central registers served few useful purposes and that they should be abolished and replaced by agency records (Corby, 1987).

Government guidance in 1988 for the first time stated more clearly that *case management* was an essential function of child protection registers (DHSS,

1988). This purpose has been re-emphasised in *Working Together Under the Children Act 1989*:

> *The purpose of the register is to provide a record of all children in the area for whom there are unresolved child protection issues and who are currently the subject of an inter-agency protection plan and to ensure that the plans are formally reviewed every six months. The register will provide a central point of speedy enquiry for professional staff who are worried about a child and want to know whether the child is the subject of an inter-agency protection plan. The register will also provide useful information for the individual child protection agencies and for the ACPC in its policy development work and strategic planning. (Home Office et al., 1991 para 6.37).*

Thus the purpose of child protection registers is not to measure the incidence and prevalence of child maltreatment. They are meant to provide a central record only of those children who have been defined by professionals from different agencies (normally with parents present and able to influence proceedings) as currently in need of an inter-agency protection plan. The central record is necessary to ensure that protection plans are regularly reviewed by all the agencies involved as well as family members. Child protection registers therefore must be fully integrated with the rest of the child protection system at local level if they are to play their part in case management.

Working Together separates the concept of a general requirement or threshold that must be reached before a child can be placed on the child protection register from the specific categories under which the registration is recorded.

> *Before a child is registered the conference must decide that there is, or is a likelihood of, significant harm leading to the need for a child protection plan. One of the following requirements needs to be satisfied:*
>
> *(i) There must be one or more identifiable incidents which can be described as having adversely affected the child. They may be acts of commission or omission. They can be either physical, sexual, emotional or neglectful. It is important to identify a specific occasion or occasions when the incident has occurred. Professional judgement is that further incidents are likely.*
>
> *or*
>
> *(ii) Significant harm is expected on the basis of professional judgement of findings of the investigation in this particular case or on research evidence. (Home Office et al., 1991 para 6.39)*

Under the Children Act 1989 harm is defined as "ill-treatment or the impairment of health or development" – including sexual abuse and non-physical ill-treatment (s. 31). The additional term *significant* introduces a higher threshold. Just when 'harm' becomes 'significant' is not entirely clear. The level at which this threshold is set has obvious implications for the operation of the child protection system. If it is set too high children who urgently need protection may be missed, but if the threshold is too low the system may become overloaded with inappropriate cases, failing to concentrate resources on children at serious risk.

The categories to be used for children on the child protection register are as follows:

Neglect: Persistent or severe neglect of a child, or the failure to protect a child from exposure to any kind of danger, including cold or starvation, or extreme failure to carry out important aspects of care, resulting in the significant impairment of the child's health or development, including non-organic failure to thrive.

Physical Injury: Actual or likely physical injury to a child, or failure to prevent physical injury (or suffering) to a child including deliberate poisoning, suffocation and Munchausen's syndrome by proxy.

Sexual Abuse: Actual or likely sexual exploitation of a child or adolescent. The child may be dependent and/or developmentally immature.

Emotional Abuse: Actual or likely severe adverse effect on the emotional and behavioural development of a child caused by persistent or severe emotional ill-treatment or rejection. All abuse involves some emotional ill-treatment. This category should be used where it is the main or sole form of abuse (Home Office et al., 1991 para 6.40).

'*Grave Concern*' as a separate category of registration (accounting for about half the registrations and cases on English registers in 1991) was abolished with the implementation of the Children Act in October, 1991. The use of this category probably contributed to confusion about the purposes of registration. By definition, all cases entered on the register are causing 'grave concern' in respect of future risk, since the criterion for registration should be the need to monitor the working of an inter-agency protection plan. Working Together, in combining actual or likely significant harm for each category of abuse, has made this clearer. The combination of a clearer definition of the child protection register's purpose, a somewhat better defined threshold and more specific categories is likely to focus minds more sharply on the evidence that must be produced at the case conference in order to demonstrate the *current* need for a protection plan.

Aims of the Study

The research was commissioned by the Department of Health in a brief which identified two main problems: wide variation in numbers of children on child protection registers in authorities of similar type; and probable wide variations in operational practices. The research was intended to provide information under three headings:

- The extent of variation in the way central registers were operated and how they were used within the child protection system;
- Variation in the processes that led to a child's name being placed on the register;
- The effects of being placed on the register.

The research was to be completed in two years.

Methods

It was decided to use a combination of a national postal survey of English registers and more detailed study in a small number of authorities. Eight Area Child Protection Committees (ACPCs) and social services departments agreed to take part. They included inner-city and suburban areas as well as counties. They were not chosen as a representative sample of English ACPCs. We approached authorities whose published register statistics suggested that we might find variations in processes and operational practices that would be illuminating. We attempted to find 'paired' ACPCs, with similar population characteristics but differing rates of children on the register and also attempted to include a mix of ACPCs with 'unusual' and more predictable rates (see Little & Gibbons, 1993). Table i sets out the small sample authorities, showing the statistics of children *on* their child protection registers and *added* to them in comparison with the average for authorities of similar type.

The results of the national postal survey carried out in the first quarter of 1991 are described in chapter two. Its purpose was to identify practices that might artificially operate to increase the rate of children on child protection registers, as well as to described more generally the way in which central registers were staffed, operated and used.

In the more detailed study undertaken in the small sample of eight authorities children referred to social services for suspected neglect or abuse were identified at the point of referral and then tracked through the system up to the point of registration, or earlier closure of the investigation. Children who were the subjects of a case conference (but not already on the register) were followed up for a further 26 weeks. Although it was originally hoped to interview key decision makers authorities generally were unable to give permission for this given the pressures on staff time. Data were collected by

Table i. **Sample Authorities: Registration Rates**

	On CPR	Added to CPR
	Rates per 1000 under 18 (1990)	
Outer London Mean	3.4	NK
OL1	4.9	2.1
OL2	3.0	1.3
Inner London Mean	8.1	NK
IL1	10.3	5.2
IL2	4.5	2.4
IL3	13.4	4.5
IL4	8.6	5.2
Counties Mean	3.6	2.2
C1	7.1	3.7
C2	2.3	2.4

Source: Children & Young Persons on Child Protection Registers Year Ending 31 March 1990. Department of Health 1991

research staff from social services records at three points in time: after the initial investigation; after the case conference; and after the 26 week follow-up.

At the time of the research, the eight social services departments in the study organised their child protection services in different ways. All except IL 3 and C 1 had at least one specialised child protection post at headquarters. IL 3 and 4 and C 2 had specialised child protection adviser or co-ordinator posts in each district or area, IL 1 had 2 such posts only and the other departments had no area-based child protection posts. C 2 in addition had a specialised child protection social work team in part of the authority. C 2 was the only authority in which the initial CP conference routinely established interagency 'core groups', often including family members, to implement the CP plan if the child was registered, but core groups were sometimes used in several of the authorities.

The questions to be examined in the more detailed study of eight authorities were:

- whether areas with high rates of children on the register would have more children referred for investigation;

- whether they would have lower thresholds: that is, investigate less 'serious' cases; and conference a higher proportion of referred children, more of whom would be placed on the register – also at lower thresholds of 'seriousness';

- whether there would be different styles of investigation and decision-making in the higher-rate authorities.

The effects of registration in the following 26 weeks were examined in terms of whether protection plans were recorded; whether legal measures and/or supportive resources were planned and actually used; whether inter-agency child protection reviews were carried out; and whether areas with high rates of children on the register showed a less active style of intervention, less clearly geared to getting children off the child protection register as early as possible. 'Outcome' of children after 26 weeks was measured by the number of repeated investigations for abuse or neglect during the follow-up period; and by whether children were removed from or remained with their own families.

A crude indicator of 'good outcome' was the proportion of children placed on the register who remained safely at home after six months. The limitations of 'administrative' outcome indicators of this type must be recognised.

Chapter 1

Variation in National Statistics of Children on Child Protection Registers

Variation and Stability over Time

Statistics from all English registers have been collected and published by the Department of Health since 1988. In each year there were wide differences between Area Child Protection Committees in rates of children *on* the register and lesser but still significant variation in rates of children *added to and removed from* the register during the year. However, the relative position of ACPCs over the period remained remarkably stable: those with high rates of children on the register in 1988 (the pilot year for national reporting) remained high in 1992 and those with low rates remained low (Pearson's correlation 1988/1991: .77). The data for the English authorities (excluding City of London and Isles of Scilly) are set out in Table 1i. Southwark, Lambeth and Camden (all Inner London authorities) remained at or near the top of the list throughout, while Gloucestershire remained at the bottom. The prevalence in 1992 ranged widely from 18.1 per thousand under 18 (Lambeth) to 0.8 per thousand (Gloucestershire). However, the high correlations between rates in different years showed that, at least in the short term, registration rates did not fluctuate randomly: the majority of authorities were using their registers in a reliable way from year to year.

Regional Variation

There is significant regional variation in the rates of children on and added to registers. In 1990 the 'prevalence' ranged from 2.1 (Thames Anglia) to 8.1 (Inner London). Although the highest-rate ACPCs were concentrated in Inner London, the regional variation remained significant even after the exclusion of Inner London, with Yorkshire & Humberside and East Midlands having higher rates. (In 1992 the Department of Health re-ordered its statistics in a way that obscures this variation).

Categories of Abuse

Authorities varied widely in the categories under which children were held on the register. For example the percentage categorised as 'Neglect' in 1990 varied from zero (Calderdale) to 38% (Isle of Wight); for 'Physical Abuse' the percentage varied from 7% (Cleveland) to 64% (Hackney); for 'Sexual Abuse' from 3% (Wandsworth) to 34% (Wolverhampton). In Trafford the rate of sexual abuse per thousand children under 18 was 0.1, while in Nottinghamshire the rate was 18 times higher (1.8 per thousand). These

Table 1.i **Rates of Children on Child Protection Registers per 1,000 under 18: England 1988–1992**

Authority	1992	1991	1990	1989	1988
Lambeth	18.1	16.4	11.1	12.0	10.4
Camden	12.4	9.8	10.3	7.9	8.0
Southwark	10.0	11.0	13.4	15.9	17.7
Wandsworth	9.9	6.8	5.2	4.5	5.3
Newcastle	8.9	8.0	7.1	6.2	6.0
Sheffield	8.6	7.2	5.4	4.9	4.3
Greenwich	8.2	9.3	10.0	11.1	8.9
Knowsley	8.0	8.6	7.4	3.2	3.2
Barnsley	7.4	6.6	5.7	NK	2.8
Islington	7.2	7.3	8.9	8.4	7.8
Notts	6.9	8.3	7.1	6.7	5.8
Wolverhampton	6.4	5.2	4.4	4.7	4.1
Liverpool	6.2	7.0	7.0	8.1	8.3
Doncaster	6.2	5.6	4.6	3.9	4.0
Calderdale	6.2	6.7	4.5	3.8	3.2
Northumberland	5.9	5.5	4.6	3.4	3.5
Coventry	5.9	5.7	4.0	3.6	4.7
Avon	5.6	7.9	9.4	7.6	NK
E Sussex	5.4	7.2	7.1	5.9	5.5
Gateshead	5.1	5.3	4.1	3.5	2.1
S Tyneside	5.0	6.2	7.0	6.1	5.8
Leeds	5.0	6.2	6.3	6.0	5.3
Sunderland	5.0	5.2	4.7	4.9	4.0
Tameside	5.0	4.9	3.8	3.4	3.9
Westminster	4.9	3.5	4.5	4.3	4.6
Birmingham	4.9	4.9	4.4	3.7	3.6
Stafford	4.9	6.2	5.9	5.3	5.0
Derbyshire	4.9	5.5	5.4	5.0	4.4
Humberside	4.9	7.5	6.9	5.8	5.4
St Helens	4.8	4.8	4.7	3.8	2.7
Wirral	4.7	4.3	3.8	3.4	2.7
Haringey	4.7	5.8	7.8	9.0	6.7
N Tyneside	4.6	5.1	5.8	6.1	5.0
Lewisham	4.5	7.0	6.6	8.4	7.8
Tower Hamlets	4.4	7.1	8.6	6.0	6.0
Rotherham	4.4	4.6	4.3	2.9	2.2
Newham	4.2	7.1	7.5	7.2	5.9
Manchester	4.2	5.6	5.3	4.9	3.8
Durham	4.1	5.1	4.6	4.5	5.1

Table 1.i **Continued**

Authority	1992	1991	1990	1989	1988
Croydon	4.1	3.7	3.4	2.6	2.3
Bexley	4.0	4.8	4.9	4.3	4.1
Hounslow	4.0	4.2	2.5	2.2	2.5
Cumbria	4.0	4.4	4.3	2.8	2.1
Hammersmith	4.0	5.5	8.1	8.1	7.6
Bolton	4.0	6.4	5.6	3.8	3.8
Bradford	3.9	6.4	8.4	8.9	8.6
Ealing	3.9	3.9	3.4	2.6	2.7
Northants	3.8	4.1	4.1	3.2	3.5
Merton	3.8	4.1	4.0	3.9	3.3
Kensington	3.7	4.8	6.5	7.5	6.2
Lincs	3.7	5.5	5.1	4.7	4.1
Dorset	3.5	4.0	3.8	4.0	3.9
Wakefield	3.5	4.4	3.6	2.8	4.1
Stockport	3.3	4.0	3.5	3.0	2.4
Cornwall	3.2	2.9	2.7	3.2	2.4
Brent	3.2	4.1	3.7	3.6	3.6
Hackney	3.1	3.5	3.0	3.7	3.7
Salford	3.1	4.7	3.3	1.6	1.4
N Yorks	3.1	4.1	3.8	2.7	2.3
Hereford	3.1	3.5	3.8	3.4	3.9
Somerset	3.0	3.4	3.1	3.0	2.8
Shropshire	3.0	5.9	5.3	6.7	6.0
Kent	3.0	3.5	3.9	4.0	6.0
Cambs	2.8	2.7	2.4	2.1	2.1
Rochdale	2.7	4.8	4.2	3.7	3.7
Kirklees	2.6	2.4	2.7	1.5	1.9
Devon	2.6	3.8	3.7	4.3	4.3
Leics	2.6	3.3	3.2	4.3	4.8
Waltham Forest	2.6	4.4	5.2	4.4	4.2
Richmond	2.5	2.5	2.8	2.6	2.4
Enfield	2.5	2.4	1.9	1.5	1.8
Oxfordshire	2.4	2.2	1.5	1.8	2.2
Sutton	2.4	2.3	2.9	1.9	2.6
Surrey	2.4	2.6	2.3	1.9	1.9
Wigan	2.4	2.9	1.7	1.2	1.5
Berkshire	2.3	3.3	3.5	3.1	2.7
Cleveland	2.3	2.4	3.1	4.1	4.4
Wiltshire	2.3	3.1	3.3	NK	NK

Table 1.i **Continued**

Authority	1992	1991	1990	1989	1988
W Sussex	2.3	2.3	2.0	1.7	1.6
Harrow	2.3	2.9	3.0	2.5	1.5
Solihull	2.2	2.4	2.4	2.7	2.6
Barking	2.2	4.0	3.3	3.0	2.3
Sefton	2.2	3.6	3.2	2.5	2.5
Oldham	2.2	2.5	2.1	2.0	1.8
Sandwell	2.0	3.4	2.6	3.8	3.6
Bromley	2.0	2.5	3.0	3.0	3.2
Lancashire	2.0	2.7	2.6	2.4	2.6
Norfolk	1.9	2.5	2.7	3.8	3.3
Cheshire	1.9	2.4	2.3	2.1	2.1
Walsall	1.9	2.6	2.1	1.2	1.6
Warwickshire	1.9	2.7	2.1	2.0	2.0
Barnet	1.8	1.4	1.6	2.2	2.6
Essex	1.8	2.5	2.1	1.9	1.8
Dudley	1.8	2.1	1.7	1.4	1.5
Bucks	1.7	1.9	1.8	1.6	1.2
Havering	1.7	2.4	1.6	1.4	1.0
Trafford	1.7	1.4	2.0	1.7	1.4
Kingston	1.7	1.7	2.7	2.0	2.8
Hillingdon	1.6	2.8	2.4	2.1	2.8
Bedfordshire	1.6	1.5	1.8	1.9	0.7
Bury	1.5	2.3	1.9	1.8	1.6
Suffolk	1.4	2.5	1.5	1.5	1.5
Isle of Wight	1.3	2.2	2.3	3.0	3.5
Hampshire	1.3	1.4	1.9	1.7	1.6
Herts	1.3	1.2	1.6	1.5	1.4
Redbridge	1.2	1.7	1.7	1.9	2.7
Gloucestershire	0.8	0.9	0.9	0.9	0.7
All	3.5	4.2	4.0	3.8	3.6

differences probably reflected the way that different authorities treated the category 'Grave Concern'. Several, such as Hackney, Dorset and Enfield, made no use at all of the category, while over a third used the category for more than half their cases – Kirklees (71%) being the extreme case. Authorities who made most use of this 'catch-all' category naturally made less use of the more specific register categories. National statistics should give a somewhat different picture in future years once 'Grave Concern' is no longer used.

Trends

Numbers of children on child protection registers in England rose from 39,200 in 1988 (the pilot year for national statistics), to 41,200 in 1989, to 43,600 in 1990 and 45,300 in 1991 – an annual increase of between four and six per cent. The rate per thousand children rose from 3.8 in 1989 to 4.2 in 1991 and the increase applied to all categories of abuse. There were no changes in national child protection procedures between 1989 and 1990 which might have accounted for the increase, but the removal of 'Grave Concern' in 1991 checked the seemingly inexorable rise and the rate fell for the first time in 1992. Between 1991 and 1992 registrations for grave concern fell by 38 per cent – against an expected fall of 50 per cent because the category was available for only half the year. Numbers on the register for grave concern fell by 39 per cent – against an expected fall of 90 per cent, showing the time-lag between issuing central guidance and its implementation. In 1992–3 approaching half the English ACPCs were still using 'Grave Concern' although the category had been officially abolished for over a year (DH, 1993).

Some idea of trends in earlier years can be gained from the NSPCC's continuous survey of children on registers maintained by it between 1983 and 1987. These registers covered 9% of the child population of England and Wales. Between 1983 and 1987 the number and rate of children on these registers doubled, due to increases in registrations for physical and sexual abuse. The NSPCC drew attention to the unclear relationship between these facts and the actual incidence of abuse, adding that, whatever the relationship, the figure had enormous resource implications for "those agencies investigating, meeting to discuss, assessing and treating the children" (Creighton & Noyes, 1989, p 45). In its final survey report, covering the period 1988–1990, the NSPCC again found large rises in the rate of children on the register (Creighton, 1992).

In summary, over the past decade (until the change resulting from abolition of 'Grave Concern'), there was a steady and continuous rise in the numbers of children officially deemed to be in need of protection and recorded on registers. However, it was not clear whether this reflected a real increase in child maltreatment, better recognition and reporting of cases, a change in thresholds so that more families were drawn into the system at lower levels of risk, or operational practices in keeping the register itself.

Differences Between Authorities: Approaches to Explanation

What factors might contribute to the stable differences between authorities in the rates of children on child protection registers? The incidence and prevalence of child maltreatment are unknown so it is impossible to know how far differences in registration rates reflect 'real' differences. In any case, child maltreatment is not the same sort of phenomenon as whooping cough: it cannot be diagnosed with scientific measuring instruments. It is more like pornography, a socially constructed phenomenon which reflects values and opinions of particular cultures at particular times (Parton, 1985). In some cultures there may be a level of tolerance for, say, the sexual use of children such that the concept of 'sexual abuse' has little meaning. Thus there may be widely differing interpretations of what constitutes 'abuse' between different authorities, even within the government's guidelines and definitions. Cultural differences in attitudes to children and differing attitudes to welfare and police authorities will also affect the public's willingness to report suspected cases.

Apart from these culturally determined definitions, it may be that in areas marked by poverty, poor housing and racial conflict whose inhabitants experience many unpleasant life events, there are more parents under stress who as a result are more likely to maltreat their children. There is evidence that variation in factors such as unemployment and the rate of births to single parents is associated with variation in rates of children on the register (Little & Gibbons, 1993). However, these factors alone do not explain much of the variance between registration rates.

Another set of explanations lies in local authority policies themselves. Some authorities may be prepared to recognise and intervene in family problems more than others. For example, Little & Gibbons found that authorities with high rates of children on the register also tended to have high rates of children in care and a large amount of day nursery provision. This may represent a certain style of responding to social deprivation and consequent stress affecting families, while other authorities in equally deprived areas may respond in a lower-key or different way.

There may be artificial factors which inflate rates of children on the register. For example, there may be purely administrative factors, such as the failure to inform the central register of the results of a case conference. Then the child's name may never be entered or never removed from the register with a consequent effect on national statistics. The rate of children *on* the register is influenced both by the rate at which children are added and the rate at which they are removed. If there is high turnover and as many children are removed as new ones are added during a year, then in theory the rate of children on the register would be the same as the rate for those added to it. However, we do not know the length of time children stay on registers nor how this varies. The 'prevalence' rate of children on the register consists of those added during the year less those removed, but plus those who have been on for a year or more. Authorities who have policies which prevent de-registration within a year will therefore have artificially inflated rates compared to others who have policies promoting more rapid turnover. However, we know that there is a significant association between rates of children on registers, rates of children added and de-registration rates, so that in general the authorities with the highest 'prevalence' rates are also the most active, with high turnover.

Differences in 'real' incidence or prevalence of child maltreatment, and differing cultural attitudes towards the child protection system were outside the scope of this research. We have tried to understand better of some of the operational practices and ACPC policies which affect the statistics. The next chapter gives a snapshot of the operation of English registers at a particular point in time – early 1991.

Chapter 2

Operational Practice in English Registers

Introduction

A postal survey of English registers was undertaken with the aims of: a) describing the extent of variation between registers in operational practices, resources and policies; and b) attempting to assess the influence of this variation on the rate of registration of children on child protection registers. The expectation was that operational and other factors would have an influence over and above the actual prevalence of children in need of inter-agency protection. The reliability of register statistics has some importance for policy, since they are important indicators in planning and allocating social services provision.

The Postal Questionnaire was circulated to 107 English registers in December, 1990 with the request that it be returned by April, 1991. The results in the main, therefore, apply to the first quarter of 1991. 90 registers returned completed Postal Questionnaires – a response rate of 84%. There was no significant difference in the response rate of counties, metropolitan districts and London boroughs.

The Postal Questionnaire was divided into 6 sections. The first 5 focussed on the operation of the register itself and questions were addressed to the Custodian. The sixth section was concerned with the organisation of the Local Authority social services department and the resources available to the child care and child protection systems. The Instructions that went out with the Postal Questionnaire stated that this section must be answered by, or with the help of, a senior social services manager with responsibilities for child care policies and resources. The largest group of respondents to the questionnaire (70%) described themselves as child protection managers. 16% were other child care, or other, managers. 2% were research staff. 9% were administrative staff. The remaining 3% did not identify their status.

National statistics of children on registers provide three measures on which Authorities can be compared: the rate of children *on* the register in a year (prevalence); the rate of children *placed* on the register in a year (incidence); and the rate of children de-registered in a year. Variation between Authorities is greatest on the prevalence measure. This measure is affected by differences in registers' procedures for entering children and for removing them. For this reason, prevalence seemed the most useful summary measure for the purposes of this study.

I. Operational and Policy Factors

Central Register Resources

There was a *custodian* in post in 82 Authorities (91% of respondents), and 90% held a CQSW. 27% had been in post for less than a year and 33% from 1 up to 3 years. Only 16% had been in post for 5 or more years. There were wide variations in the level at which the custodian post was graded. Apart from the custodian, the *number of additional staff* employed full-time on the central register ranged from 0 to 7, with a mean of just under 1. The number of part-timers ranged from 0 to 5, with a mean of 1.2. 16 Authorities reported unfilled vacancies for central register staff. The majority of respondents (72% of those who answered the question) considered there were enough staff to maintain an up-to-date register. There were regional variations in the number of staff employed, with East Midlands above, and West Midlands, Thames Anglia and London below the average.

Table 2.i shows the extent to which the registers had been computerised. Altogether, almost two-thirds were already computerised and of the remainder, all but one register reported plans to become so.

Table 2.i. **Computerisation of Registers**

	Number	%
MainFrame/Mini	20	22
PC	32	36
Both	2	2
Computerised, No Particulars	5	6
Not Computerised	31	34
All	90	100

Computerised registers did not report using any fewer staff on average, but they were less likely to complain of insufficient staff. It may be that computerisation reduces the demands on staff and allows more effective operation.

Most computerised registers reported that they were using specially commissioned data management systems, from their own Authority (40%), bought in from another Local Authority (26%), from an outside consultancy (15%) and from other or unknown sources (19%). The data management systems provided various functions (Table 2.ii).

Nearly half of those who had computerised reported no problems with their systems, while only 4% reported that they had many problems. Some respondents commented that computerisation worked best when the system

Table 2.ii. **Functions Provided by Computerised Systems**

	% Providing Function
Entering Data	100
Editing Data	100
Listing according to Specific Conditions	94
DoH Statistics	86
Other Statistics	94
Prompting for Reviews	78
Other Function	40
BASE NUMBER: COMPUTERISED REGISTERS ANSWERING QUESTION	50

took account of the needs of the child protection system as a whole. It should not be used only for the production of statistics but as part of a general management system, for example by printing out address labels for those invited to Case Conferences, printing out Decision Sheets, and so on. By this means clerical staff also gained something from the introduction of the new system and were motivated to use it.

Data Held On Central Registers

Half the registers reported using a standardised data entry form. Table 2.iii shows the data held on registers. There was significant variation by type of Authority, with Inner London ones holding least and Metropolitan Districts most. 80% of Authorities reported that data were regularly updated, while 20% reported 'sometimes' updating. 19% were 'Very Confident' of the accuracy of their data, 59% were 'Confident', 16% were unsure and only 7% were 'Not Very Confident'. There was no variation by type of Authority, nor according to whether or not the register was computerised, but registers with 'Insufficient' staff and those who could not upddate regularly tended to express less confidence. Some respondents pointed out that problems in maintaining accurate data could be due to the failure of social work staff in area offices to notify the central register of changes, as well as to shortages of staff at particular times.

Eleven registers reported having an intermediate category between 'Active Registration' and 'De-registration' on which they held data, and two more probably had such a category. Thus not all the children on these registers were the subjects of active protection plans. One or two reported that they were creating a new Intermediate category for children who had been abused but were not felt to need a protection plan. Just over a third of the registers reported that children could be placed on the register before birth,

Table 2.iii. **Data Held on Central Registers**

	% Holding Item	
	All Cases	**Some Cases**
Name/Address of child	100	
Child's sex	93	2
Child's DOB	98	1
Child's birthplace	22	17
Child's current location	96	3
Child's legal status: entry	74	11
Current legal status	80	10
Carers' Names	90	6
Other Adults in HH	64	19
Regular adult visitors	26	37
Carers' criminal record	22	36
Other criminal records	13	38
Other children in HH	86	6
Other children DOB	82	6
Other children sex	78	6
Other children legal status	47	13
Other children on CPR	87	2
First ref for abuse	64	9
Key worker details	97	1
GP details	79	7
Health Visitor details	64	16
Teacher details	53	13
Other agency details	66	18
Referral source	66	9
Date registered	96	1
Date carers told	33	11
Review programme	40	8
Date next review	73	6
Date last review	74	2
Date de-registration	94	—
Reason registered	62	1
New office if moved	70	10
BASE NUMBER	90	

and another 10 had similar arrangement. Twelve registers (14%) reported that the names of children who died were kept on the register and those children were included in statistical returns.

Criteria for Entry to Registers

It seemed likely that differing criteria would be an important source of variation between registers. However, it proved particularly difficult to frame questions about criteria for registration and de-registration which would be understood in the same way by all respondents. Many local authority child protection staff think of 'criteria' as synonymous with 'Department of Health registration categories'. In trying to distinguish between the two, the Notes to respondents that accompanied the Questionnaire explained:

> *'Criteria' . . . are not the same as the <u>categories</u> under which children are registered. 'Criteria' refer to general rules governing the entry of children to the register. Such rules, for example, might specify the level of risk, or the degree of certainty of risk, or the need for an inter-agency plan, that must exist before a child can be registered under any of the categories.*

In spite of this guidance, over a third of respondents answered the questions, "Please list the criteria used by your authority for placing a child on the Child Protection Register" simply by reference to the Department of Health registration categories, or to an earlier version of them. These answers suggest that approaching 40% of authorities had not formulated any general criteria governing registration.

Among those authorities which had formulated criteria, the most commonly used was that the *need for an inter-agency protection plan* be established before registration could occur. One metropolitan district, for example, replied:

> *Registration will occur when a Case Conference concludes that: a) Abuse is confirmed or strongly suspected or potential abuse is identified <u>AND</u> b) An inter-agency child protection plan is regarded as necessary for the welfare of the child.*

Altogether, 41 respondents (45%) indicated that the need for an inter-agency plan to protect the child had to be established before registration. In these authorities there was an explicit policy statement that abuse was not enough by itself: there had to be some assessment in the case conference of the nature and degree of risk to the child that still existed and whether this was sufficient to require an inter-agency protection plan. Metropolitan Districts were significantly more likely than other types of Local Authority to use this criterion.

A few authorities had developed other general criteria. One or two counties, for example, had recently revised their criteria to take account of the changes introduced by the Children Act (1989). Two counties had very similar formulations:

i) There has been significant and avoidable lack of care displayed towards the child by parent or carer, through commission or omission. It is important to be able to identify specific instances or instance

AND

ii) The harm is currently demonstrable and/or confidently expected on the basis of professional judgment or research evidence

AND

iii) A causal link has been established between parent/caregiving behaviour and identified harm to the child or the behaviour is such that harm will very likely occur.

One or two authorities had established quite restrictive criteria for registration. For example, one required that grounds for Care proceedings under s. 1(2) a, b, bb, c could be proven or that grounds existed for the High Court to issue a summons, *and* there was a pragmatic need for a protection plan, *and* that registration would not be counter-productive. In another metropolitan district not only had there to be continuing risk justifying the need for a protection plan, but also, for neglect, emotional abuse and grave concern there had to be "evidence that the grounds for care proceedings may be met and the level of concern is such that unless the situation improves significantly over a relatively short time scale then care proceedings are likely to be initiated".

Two thirds of respondents reported revising their criteria within the last two years, and 80% had revised them in the last three years. Three-quarters believed that the present entries on their registers reflected a mix of past and present criteria. Since revision of criteria in the light of changing policy must be a continuing process, there will perhaps never be a time when registers are entirely internally consistent.

Categories of Registration

Nearly all respondents said they used the Department of Health main registration categories. Fewer used the 'mixed' categories. 41% reported using other categories in addition to or instead of the main ones (Table 2.iv). The one register that was not using the category '*Neglect*' was managed by the NSPCC and was about to be taken over by the Local Authority, when the systems would change. This register was not using the category '*Emotional Abuse*'. The other register not using this category was also managed by the

Table 2.iv. **Registration Categories Used**

Category	% Respondents Using Category
Neglect	99
Physical Abuse	100
Sexual Abuse	100
Emotional Abuse	98
Grave Concern	93
Neglect + Physical + Sexual	80
Neglect + Physical	82
Neglect + Sexual	82
Physical + Sexual	82
Other Category	41
BASE NUMBER	90

NSPCC and in a state of transition. It seems that in the near future all registers will be using the four main categories and, in most cases, employing written definitions which will help in maintaining consistency.

'Grave Concern' differs from the four main categories in that it does not refer to a *type* of abuse, but rather a *degree* of risk. Six Authorities reported not using 'Grave Concern'. In some cases this was probably due to the register's being in a transitional state, but two reported a deliberate decision. In one county, the ACPC had agreed to omit 'Grave Concern' on the grounds that it "was not clearly defined. It appears to attract a high degree of registration across the country but we felt it could lead to a lack of clarity concerning the reasons for registration." One authority reported "We do not like the DoH categories, in particular the Grave Concern Category". One Metropolitan District had its own definition: "Lifestyle places children at risk". The grounds were further defined as "Inadequate explanation of injury; Suspicion of sexual abuse; Unexplained failure to thrive due to neglect/emotional neglect; Live in the same household as another child who has been abused." The London Authorities (and one or two others) had agreed a common definition of 'Grave Concern' which was intended to avoid its becoming a catch-all category:

> *Grave concern reflects a high degree of risk, substantiated by social and/or medical assessments, where there are no grounds for stating that abuse has already taken place.*
>
> *This concern* <u>must</u> *state the form of abuse (as defined by the 4 main categories) of which the child is felt to be at risk and may include those situations where another child in the household has been harmed or where*

the household contains a known abuser. It must <u>not</u> be used as a catch-all category.

Thirty-two respondents (35%) stated their registers used *additional categories*. Fifteen listed '*Non-organic Failure to Thrive*' as a separate category, rather than combining it with 'Neglect'. Ten listed '*Child in Same Household as Person Previously Involved in Abuse*'. One county used '*Ritualistic*', and another listed '*Substance Abuse*', where this posed risk to the child. The remainder did not state which particular additional categories were used. Many registers who used additional or alternative categories translated them for the Department of Health returns.

Respondents were asked whether *other children in the household* of a registered child were automatically placed on the register. Only four said that they were. However another 17 (19%) said other children were 'sometimes' registered.

There was considerable variation in policy towards *dual registration* – maintaining a child on the registers of more than one Authority. In 34% there was a definite policy to do this; in 32% it sometimes happened; and in just over 33% it was avoided.

In just under a quarter consideration was being given to the inclusion of separate categories for *Organised Abuse* and *Institutional Abuse*.

Thirty five respondents (39%) stated that they found 'some' *difficulty in using the Department of Health categories* and another 4% experienced 'considerable' difficulties. Much the most common reason for difficulty was the "vagueness", "wooliness", "over-inclusiveness", "difficulty of defining" Grave Concern: this problem was mentioned by 19 respondents (21% of the total). However, only three of the 26 London respondents, whose Authorities had agreed a tighter definition of this category, complained of difficulty in its use. The next most common reason for difficulty was the 'mixed' categories, and the need to decide on a primary category, mentioned by 13 respondents (14% of the total). One Authority felt that there was inconsistency in the definition of Physical and Sexual Abuse, with 'reasonable suspicion' being allowed for in relation to the former but not the latter, where it was more relevant. Another Authority felt that the categories were insufficiently directed to the issue of future harm. A few sought further guidance on appropriate thresholds – especially in distinguishing between physical abuse and excessive chastisement.

Criteria for Removal from the Register

The questionnaire attempted to establish to what extent registers were developing rules under which children could be routinely taken off the register, without the need for individual consideration at a Case Conference.

The great majority did not formulate general rules for the removal of children from the register in specified circumstances (such as following a Care Order, or the removal of the perpetrator) and virtually none allowed for de-registration without individual review by a case conference, except in the limited circumstances of the child's reaching 17 or 18, moving permanently out of the area, or in a few Authorities, being placed in permanent substitute care. However, some Authorities, particularly those still managed by the NSPCC, allowed for review by post, whereby details were circulated to case conference members who had to reply, but did not have to meet face to face. In the great majority, however, de-registration was only permissible when a child protection review decided that the original grounds for concern no longer applied and the child was no longer at risk.

Forty-seven per cent believed that inter-agency reviews held up de-registration, most often because of difficulties in securing attendance.

Two-thirds said they had policies governing the length of time data would be kept after de-registration. Less than a third of these kept data for five or more years. About half said that some analysis had been done of the length of time children remained on their registers, but only 21% felt that the data were in a fit state to be made available to DoH statisticians.

Table 2.v. **Specialist Organisation in Responding Authorities**

Specialist Organisation	% Respondents	
Children & Families Teams:		
Generally	52	
In some Areas	20	
Child Protection Teams:		
Generally	10	
In some Areas	18	
Child Protection Posts:		
Headquarters only:	33	
District/Area only:	19	
HQ and District:	36	
None:	5	
Other:	7	
Mean Advisory Posts	2.3	Range 0–15
Mean Management Posts	.9	Range 0–7
Mean Social Work Posts	2.7	Range 0–28
BASE NUMBER	90	

Table 2.vi. **Availability of Family Support Resources**

Resource	Unavailable	Restricted	Short Supply
		% Respondents	
LA Nursery	10	4	52
Other Nursery	4	1	44
Child Minding	—	—	20
Playgroup	—	—	21
Day Fostering	22	8	38
SW Allocation	—	4	49
Family Aide	9	13	45
BASE NUMBER	90		

Local Authority Policies and Resources

This section of the Questionnaire attempted to gather information about policies and resource issues which might influence operation of the register. These were the degree of specialisation and the number of specialised child protection staff employed; and policies regarding the use of family support resources, such as nurseries, day fostering, family aides. It was possible that authorities which restricted the use of certain resources to children on the register might create an incentive for staff to register more children. The degree of specialisation is shown in Table 2.v.

Limited availability of a range of family support resources is illustrated in Table 2.vi. 'Unavailable' means that the respondent stated that there was no such resource. 'Restricted' means that the Authority's policy was that the resource could be used only by children on the register or subject to statutory Orders. 'Short Supply' means that there were no policy restrictions on use of the resource, but its availability was limited because it was scarce.

Influence of Operational and Policy Factors on Registration

What effect did variation in operational practices, policies and resources have on rates of children on the register? A number of the factors examined were *not* found to have any association with rates of children on the register. These were:

● Absence of general criteria for entry to the register

● Recency of revision of criteria

● Inclusion of unborn on register

● Inclusion of other children in the household

● Number of DoH categories used

● Use of written definitions of categories

- Use of categories other than those recommended by the DoH
- Dual registration policy
- Allocation to a social worker a condition of registration
- Past criteria still influencing composition of the register
- Use of 'inactive' category
- Policy to remove if Care Order made
- Policy to remove if perpetrator leaves household
- Number of unfilled posts on central register
- Number of specialised child protection posts
- 'Enough' staff to maintain register

Eleven factors, however, were found to show a significant association (or there was a strong trend towards association) with rates of children on the register. These were:

- Inclusion of dead children
- Need for protection plan not stated as criterion for entry to the register
- Specific criteria (other than absence of risk) for de-registration
- Delay in de-registration caused by review procedures
- No regular updating of register
- Respondent not confident of accuracy of register data
- Decentralised pattern of overall organisation
- Specialised child protection posts at HQ not area offices
- Restricted family support resources
- Family support resources in short supply
- Respondent named factor raising rate

The first four variables reflect definitions and criteria used by a particular register. If a register had policies which mandated the inclusion of dead children's names; if there was no general statement that a necessary condition for entry to the register was the need for an inter-agency protection plan; if there was a specific criterion – such as the absence of the perpetrator – for removing a child's name from the register rather than a more general criterion that there was no longer a risk to the child; or if there were said to be procedural delays in removing children's names – such as rules which prevented removal within a year – there were more children on the register.

The next two variables (failure to update regularly and inaccurate data) probably reflect resource problems which caused registers to become out of date: children's names might have remained on the register for longer in this type of area due to administrative inefficiency or pressures caused by lack of clerical resources.

The next four variables reflect aspects of the organisation of Children and Families' services which were apparently associated with high rates of children on the register. The trend for decentralised Authorities to have higher rates might be due to weaker central monitoring systems in that type of authority, or to inadequate information flow between the centre and the decentralised areas – for example, children might be de-registered in the areas and the central register not informed. It is suggestive that the lack of 'preventive' family support resources appeared to be associated with maintaining more children on the register. In this type of area there might have been an incentive to place children on the register and keep them there so as to secure their families' access to limited family support resources.

The combined effect was tested by allotting an arbitrary score of '1' to each factor: each register then had a possible score of 0 to 11, depending on how many of the factors applied in its case. This was the Operational Factors Index. In other words, registers with high Index scores had many of these operational practices, resource factors and policies, while registers which scored low did not. The correlation between scores on the Operational Factors Index and the rate of children *on* the register in 1990 was .58. The correlation with the rate of children *placed* on the register was .424, and with the de-registration rate was .310. Table 2.vii shows the 20 registers with the highest (1990) rate, and the 20 lowest, with their scores on the Operational Factors Index. The mean score of the 20 high-rate registers was 7.05, while the mean score for the 20 lowest rate registers was 3.5. However, there was by no means a perfect correspondence. Some high-rate Authorities, such as Avon and Tower Hamlets, had fairly low Operational Factors Index scores, and one low-rate Authority (Surrey) had many operational factors. Nonetheless, it did appear that the policies and practices included in the Operational Factors Index, when considered together, were having an effect on the numbers of children on the register.

II. Uses of the Central Register

Respondents' Views

Respondents were first asked the general question 'How essential is the central Register to the implementation of your Authority's child protection policy?' Table 2.viii shows that 80% considered the Register to be an essential part of the child protection system.

Integration of Registers in Local Child Protection Systems

One way of testing how far the central register is integrated into the rest of the child protection system is to see whether it is used to maintain regular

Table 2.vii. **Operational Factors Index: 20 Highest Registration Rate and 20 Lowest Rate Authorities**

Highest Rate	Reg. Rate	OFI	Lowest Rate	Reg. Rate	OFI
Camden	10.3	8	Glos	0.9	5
Avon	9.4	4	Suffolk	1.5	2
Islington	8.9	6	Oxfordshire	1.5	2
Tower Hamlets	8.6	4	Havering	1.6	2
Hamersmith	8.1	8	Barnet	1.6	5
Newham	7.5	7	Herts	1.6	5
Knowsley	7.4	10	Redbridge	1.7	3
East Sussex	7.1	7	Enfield	1.7	3
Notts	7.1	7	Wigan	1.7	5
Newcastle	7.1	8	Dudley	1.7	4
Liverpool	7.0	6	Bucks	1.8	2
S Tyneside	7.0	7	Beds	1.8	3
Humberside	6.9	7	Bury	1.9	3
Lewisham	6.6	6	Hants	1.9	4
Kensington	6.5	9	Trafford	2.0	4
Leeds	6.3	8	W Sussex	2.0	2
Staffs	5.9	8	Warwicks	2.1	2
N Tyneside	5.8	7	Surrey	2.3	7
Barnsley	5.7	6	I O Wight	2.3	2
Bolton	5.6	8	Cambs	2.4	3

Note: Non-respondents and registers not publishing 1990 statistics were excluded.

Table 2.viii. **Respondents' Views of the Value of the Central Register in the Child Protection System**

Value	Number	%
Essential (Unqualified)	61	68
Essential (Qualified)	11	12
Unsure	6	7
Probably/Certainly Inessential	7	8
Did Not Answer	5	5
ALL	90	100

Table 2.ix. **Enquiries to the Central Register during 6 Months**

Type of Authority	Mean Enquiries	SD	Range
Countries (29)	429	406.8	1–1214
Met. Districts (23)	261	354.5	5–1591
Inner London (6)	48	39.5	5–108
Outer London (14)	108	100	9–277

reviews of children on the register. 49% of respondents said that the operation of their child protection reviews depended on the central register, and another 21% said that some use was made of the register to maintain CP reviews. Thus the central register was used to support regular child protection reviews in approaching three-quarters of authorities.

Another way of testing the usefulness of the central register is by counting the enquiries made to it. Four fifths of respondents were able to provide the total number of enquiries made in a six-month period, though fewer identified the source of enquiries. The mean number of enquiries made (to 72 Authorities) over 6 months was 281. The range was huge – from 1 to 1591. However, only seven Authorities reported receiving less than 10 enquiries; while 14 received from 10 to 49; 30 received 50 to 99; 30 received 100 to 499; and 15 received 500 or more. Numbers of enquiries are obviously heavily influenced by size and type of authority. Table 2.ix illustrates the results for different types of Authority. There were wide variations even within types, which may be due to different practices of recording enquiries, or may reflect actual differences in the number of enquiries.

The registers were most used by enquirers from within the social services department, with a mean 149 enquiries in the previous 6 months (range 0–998). Health-based professionals made a mean 21 enquiries (range 0–244); education-based professionals a mean 13 enquiries (range 0–289); other social services departments a mean 11 enquiries (range 0–109) and other sources, such as probation, a mean 48 enquiries (range 0–361).

Since it was possible that the number of enquiries to the central register reflected the levels of inter-agency co-operation that existed locally, respondents were asked to rate co-operation with other agencies as 'Excellent', 'Good', 'Fair' or 'Poor'. The results are illustrated in Table 2.x. Co-operation with the police and health visitors was generally problem-free. The great majority had co-operative relations with education and hospital staff, and over half with the NSPCC. Relations with general practitioners were the exception, with only 17% of respondents rating them as co-operative. Levels of co-operation did not affect the reported number of enquiries.

Table 2.x. **Respondents' Views of Inter-Agency Co-operation**

Agency	% Rating Excellent/Good
Police	93
Health Visitors	85
Education	77
Hospital Staff	72
NSPCC	57
General Practitioners	17
BASE NUMBER	90

Most respondents gave reasons for their belief that the central register was essential to the implementation of local child protection policies. Mentioned most often, by 54% of those who considered the register essential, was its use as a *management information* system. Quarterly or other statistics were produced which formed the basis for planning services, deciding on resource allocation, and which were used as performance indicators in quality assurance systems. Consistency between different areas was maintained through register monitoring systems. Examples illustrate these functions.

> It is a source of quantifiable information which is used to demonstrate to senior managers and to the social services committee the weight of the workload. Increase in numbers registered in the child sexual abuse category added impetus to a joint funding bid for the equivalent of one full-time post for the treatment of sexually abused children and their families (Outer London borough).

> It serves a number of management purposes e.g. HQ monitoring and quality assurance; sustaining claims under Criminal Injuries Compensation scheme; statistical analysis (County).

> All children in Care require Director's consent prior to allowing unsupervised access/overnight stays/rehabilitation. The CPR co-ordinates this (County).

> Increases in registrations in particular Areas or teams can be investigated, as can variations in categories of registration between Areas. Trends in registration categories influences both training programmes and service planning (County).

Next often mentioned, by 42%, was the register's value in *supporting child protection practice.*

It provides the fulcrum for monitoring and review of individual cases (Metropolitan District).

Ensuring there are plans, reviews and work to de-registration (County).

The register's use in maintaining *inter-agency co-ordination* overall and in relation to particular cases was specifically mentioned by 26%. 16% referred specifically to its use as an "alerting mechanism" in operating checks and responding to enquiries, especially for Emergency Duty Teams.

The 13 respondents who stated that the register was not essential to their systems also gave reasons. In several cases the main reason was the cumbersome nature of the present manual system, which was to be replaced by a computerised one. Others felt that the register would not produce uniformity or protection of itself. One respondent stated that child protection work was subsumed within the general field of Children and Families work so that separate policies were not needed.

Conclusion

The postal survey of English registers achieved a satisfactory response rate (84%) and appeared reasonably representative of different types of Local Authority. It is possible, however, that registers experiencing the most difficulties were the least likely to reply. One or two non-respondent custodians explained that pressures were such that they could not complete the Questionnaire, even when extra time was allowed. The survey was carried out in 1991, before the implementation of the Children Act, 1989 and the publication of revised government guidance. Many registers may have already updated their procedures to take account of these changes.

In general, the majority of registers appeared to be working well, with sufficient resources for custodians to feel confident about the accuracy of data. New technology was being widely used and will be almost universally used in the next few years. Late comers to new technology may well develop the most efficient systems. However, approaching 20% of registers were in considerable difficulties because of staff shortages and lack of resources.

80% of respondents felt that the register was an essential part of the Authority's child protection system, and there was evidence of the registers' integration into the operation of the child protection system at local level. For example, the technical facilities of the registers were being used to support the case conference and review process. Managers who gave reasons for their belief that registers were essential most often adduced their function in providing management information. They also referred to the registers' value in supporting child protection practice; in dealing with emergencies; and in promoting inter-agency co-operation. There was evidence that registers were being extensively used by enquirers from within the social services and, to a lesser extent, from other agencies to make checks on children. Only seven registers had received less than 10 enquiries in the previous six months, and the majority had received over 100. Thus, the evidence from this survey would not support those who argue that there is no need to keep central registers since they fulfil no useful functions.

However, there were wide variations between registers in resources, operational practices and policies. Variation was particularly noticeable in the use of general criteria for entry to the register, and in the actual categories under which children were registered. Physical and sexual abuse were the only categories used by 100% of informants. There were also differences and difficulties in interpreting the categories and in deciding on appropriate thresholds. The category 'Grave Concern' was causing most difficulty and a few ACPCs had taken a deliberate decision not to use it. Since the survey, the category 'Grave Concern' has been abolished. While this will solve some problems, it will now be impossible to distinguish between cases involving actual abuse and cases where abuse is considered to be a risk for various reasons but no actual incident has occurred. An alternative solution might have been found in the general adoption of the London common criteria, listed on page 20, which included 'Grave Concern', but tied it to one of the main categories. This would allow cases registered for physical injury, for example, to be divided into those where injury had actually occurred and those where it was feared.

It could be argued that all children placed on the register are by definition the subjects of grave concern, since the criterion for entry should be the need to monitor the working of an inter-agency protection plan in respect of a child who is in continuing danger. Thus a register does not record all children who are known to have experienced abuse, but only those who are at continuing risk and in need of inter-agency protection. There appeared to be some differences between authorities in their understanding of the fundamental purpose of the register: some still saw it as a record of documented abuse in the past, rather than as part of a monitoring system focussed on the immediate future. A few Authorities, for example, were maintaining an 'Intermediate' group of cases on the register for whom there were no protection plans, and others maintained the names of dead children.

There was less stated variation in criteria for removing children from the register. Most Authorities had no specific criteria but depended on the judgment of the child protection review conference that the child was no longer at risk. Here, the problem was more one of procedural delays in removing children's names.

The reported variations in resources, practices and policies had a marked effect on the statistics of children on the register in 1990. Because they operate to different policies and use different criteria it is difficult to compare statistics of children on registers in different areas. Because of this unreliability, national register statistics should not be treated as accurate indicators of the 'true' incidence and prevalence of children in need of protection in different communities. Nor should they be used as valid indicators of trends in the occurrence of child abuse over time: we could not conclude from a rise in the rate of children on registers that there had been a real increase in child abuse, nor would a drop in registrations mean a real decrease in incidence.

We believe, nonetheless, that child protection registers in some form should continue, as 'central records' available to all the agencies concerned. The great majority of respondents saw them as useful parts of local systems to improve the detection and prevention of child abuse. Without the registers even less would be known about how agencies are carrying out their duties in child protection and, in that sense, their existence increases openness and accountability. However, the value of national register statistics for planning and policy-making would be increased if firmer central guidance were given to standardise criteria, categories and definitions.

Chapter 3

Entry to the Child Protection System in Eight Authorities

The Authorities Taking Part in the Research

The rationale determining the choice of authorities for the study of child protection referrals has been explained in the introduction, but a little more descriptive detail may help the reader at this point. Table 3i shows some basic information. There were two Outer London boroughs (OL 1 and 2), mainly suburban areas without much social deprivation, with OL 1 having a higher rate of children on the register. Of the four Inner London boroughs, IL 1 and 2 were inner city areas both of which included extremes of wealth and poverty, while Boroughs 3 and 4 were among the most deprived areas in the country. IL 1 and 3 had high rates of children on the register compared with IL 2 and 4. The two counties were situated within 50 miles of each other in the midlands and both included large urban areas as well as rural hinterlands. All the authorities with higher rates on the register also had higher rates of children in care, in conformity with the national relationship between these two variables.

Method of Identifying Children

Before the research began, we identified with the help of managers in our eight authorities all the 'sites' (social work teams in area, hospital or other settings) to which suspected cases of child abuse and neglect might be initially referred for investigation. We then approached staff at all these sites to seek

Table 3i. **Features of the 8 Research Authorities**

Authority	Resident Population	Age 0–4 %	Age 5–15 %	Sg Par %	Standard Deprivation Score 'z'	Children In Care per 10,000 <18
OL 1	215,615	6.9	13.2	4.3	−1.82	38
OL 2	200,100	6.5	13.5	4.3	−0.33	21
IL 1	170,444	5.7	10.4	6.8	4.05	95
IL 2	174,814	5.0	8.6	5.7	2.97	90
IL 3	218,541	7.9	12.5	8.9	4.4	131
IL 4	161,064	9.1	16.5	8.0	5.53	101
C 1	993,872	6.7	13.3	5.4	−3.23	86
C 2	956,616	6.6	13.9	4.8	−2.32	43

Source: Census 1991 County Monitors and Department of Health (1990) Key Indicators of LA Social Services

their co-operation in the research. All the relevant sites in six of the eight research authorities agreed to take part. In IL4, however, staff in one of the nine sites were on strike when the research began and so this site had to be omitted. In IL1 all staff went on strike during the research, causing the period when cases were identified for the research to be cut from 16 to 12 weeks, and the omission of one site where industrial action started prematurely.

During an intake period of 16 weeks, children were notified to the research by senior social workers on standard forms. All children were to be notified who met the following criteria:

- Under 16 on date of referral

- Had an address in the local authority area

- Were first-ever referrals
  OR
  Re-referrals of cases previously known to the department
  OR
  New episodes of abuse/neglect in cases already open for whatever reason
  AND

- The question must arise in the duty officer's or senior's mind that child protection issues requiring investigation may be involved.

The final criterion was deliberately unspecific since we were interested in possible different 'thresholds' for entry to the system: a case that was considered to raise child protection issues in one authority might not do so in another.

A research worker visited each site regularly to collect the forms, deal with any problems and encourage compliance with the research procedures. The researchers had access to social work records of the referral and the subsequent investigation and transcribed data onto standard forms. In C2, where there were some delays in negotiating access, shortage of resources made us unable to abstract all the data from three of the sites who notified children.

Who Entered the Child Protection System?

Table 3ii shows the numbers of children notified to the research in the eight different authorities. An estimated referral rate for an average four weeks is shown in the third column. Inner London boroughs had markedly higher referral rates. Within the 'paired' authorities, OL 1 and C 1 (high register rate authorities) had somewhat higher referral rates than OL 2 and C 2. However IL 1 and IL 3 (high register rate authorities) did *not* have higher referral rates than IL 2 and IL 4. High official registration rates, therefore, are unlikely to be explained simply in terms of greater numbers of children referred to the system.

Table 3ii. **Children Notified to the Research from 8 Authorities**

Authority	Pop. 0–15	Notified in 16 Wk	Estimated 4 Wk Referral Rate per 1000 <16	On CPR 1990 per 1000<18
OL 1	43,338	202 (140)	1.16	4.9
OL 2	40,020	158 (115)	0.99	3.0
IL 1[1]	27,441	147 (125)	1.78	10.3
IL 2	23,774	172 (138)	1.81	4.5
IL 3	44,582	269 (191)	1.51	13.4
IL 4[2]	41,232	256 (192)	1.55	8.6
C 1	198,774	905 (676)	1.14	7.1
C 2[3]	192,279	649 (438)	0.84	2.3

Number of families in brackets
Sources: OPCS, 1991 Census County Monitors
         Department of Health, Children & Young Persons on Child Protection Registers: England
[1] Notification period reduced to 12 weeks and one office excluded, both due to strikes
[2] One office excluded due to strike
[3] 311 of the 438 families notified were followed in the research

Reasons for Notification

There were significant differences between the research authorities in the type of child maltreatment identified (Table 3iii). (Notifications for emotional abuse are not illustrated because so few children were notified for emotional abuse alone – less than 3 %). In general, the authorities with higher rates of children on the register identified a higher proportion of children as warranting investigation for possible sexual abuse, and a lower proportion as raising concerns about physical neglect or safety issues – such as the child being left alone in the house. Physical abuse concerns were equally likely to be identified in high and low rate authorities.

Severity: Neglect

Referrals for *neglect* were categorised into allegations solely of children being left alone, and allegations of physical or other forms of neglect (which sometimes also included leaving children alone). 'Left alone' usually involved a less serious level of alleged neglect. In 26 %, the referrals were solely on account of children being left alone.

Table 3iii. **Reasons for Notification of Children in the Research Authorities**

Authority	Physical	Sexual	Neglect	Safety
		% children notified		
OL 1	29	24	26	18
OL 2	40	15	28	25
IL 1	45	29	25	24
IL 2	40	16.5	32	22
IL 3	40.5	29	20	13
IL 4	45	21	27.5	24
C 1	43	30	17	15
C 2	36	18.5	33	24

Note: Some children were notified under more than one reason and are included under each. Percentages do not sum to 100.

Example [1].

A child (4) living with a single parent was referred by a neighbour who alleged that the child was often left alone, was allowed out unsupervised and had been seen putting her hand through a broken window upstairs trying to climb out. Caller insisted that SSD do something, otherwise neighbours will take action (case 801: neglect plus left alone).

Severity: Physical Injury

Severity of physical injuries was categorised under four headings: injuries were considered more serious if they were inflicted by more than a slap (that is, by a punch, kick, shake, throw or instrument); if they left more than a bruise (that is a cut, burn, fracture etc in addition to a bruise); if they produced physical consequences likely to last more than two weeks; and finally, if they had fatal consequences. Table 3iv shows the proportion of cases with more serious injuries, using these definitions. Although nearly two-thirds of investigations involved more than a slap, in about four-fifths bruising only was the result.

Examples

Father hit child (13) five or six times round head with slipper, causing black eye, after child defied him, returning over two hours late at night (case 91: more than a slap).

A 12 year old girl was taken to hospital with a cut finger caused when father drunkenly threatened to commit suicide by sticking the knife into his chest (case 610: more than a bruise).

---

[1] Examples throughout the text are randomly chosen by research number.

Table 3iv. **Severity of Physical Injury**

Authority	More than a slap	More than a bruise	Consequences over 2 Wks	Fatal
		% cases referred for physical injury		
OL 1	72	29	9	0
OL 2	52	13	0	0
IL 1	79	25	7	2.1
IL 2	60	17	9	1.7
IL 3	66	24	7	0
IL 4	83	44	4	0
C 1	57	15	1	0.3
C 2	60	23	7	0.8
All (%)	64	22	4	0.5

BASE NO. = 823 cases. Missing data on 16 cases

Mother reported that cohabitee had slapped child on leg after child boasted about drinking alcohol on access visit to natural father. No marks were visible (case 101: slap).

Only 4 % involved injuries with more serious longer-term consequences. There were marked differences between authorities. For example, in OL 2 nearly half the alleged injuries were relatively trivial (a slap or less) compared to less than a quarter in IL 4. Thus there did appear to be different thresholds for investigation, but there was no clear tendency for high rate authorities to display lower thresholds of severity.

Fatal Injuries

Four children were notified with fatal injuries and there was one further possible death, regarded as a cot death but one in which old injuries were found at post mortem.

Case 305 was a 6 week old baby whose mother was a lone parent living in a mother and baby hostel. Two previous children had been taken into care and placed for adoption after confirmed allegations of neglect. The mother brought the baby to hospital where he was found to be dead. He was placed on a ventilator but there was no evidence of brain activity. His heart had stopped in unclear circumstances and it was believed that his feed might have entered the lungs. He also appeared to have a broken arm. There was no inquest and child protection procedures were not proceeded with as the death was considered to be from natural causes.

Case 929 was another baby who presented at hospital with brain damage and died soon afterwards. Death was subsequently found to be due to damage in utero from the mother's use of drugs.

Case 1232 was a 3 week old baby who was brought to casualty pale and apparently lifeless. Examination showed at least 5 fractures of the ribs of varying ages and severe brain damage probably from shaking. The baby was severely under-nourished. The father was subsequently charged with murder.

In case 2033 the researcher was not permitted access to the full file. A 17 month old baby was admitted unconscious to hospital with a skull fracture and other injuries and later died. The explanation of "a fall" was not considered consistent with the injuries and the mother's cohabitee was arrested and charged. Later it emerged that the baby had been admitted before with "possible NAI concerns". Child protection procedures had not been followed by the hospital on that occasion.

Severity: Sexual Abuse

Cases referred for sexual abuse were classified into one of 7 categories. In 21% there was no report of any signs or symptoms but some risk was alleged, such as contact with a Schedule 1 offender. In 4% there was a medical symptom, such as a vaginal discharge, but no specific allegation. In 15 % suspicions had been aroused by a behaviour change in the child, without any other evidence. In 4 % the allegation involved looking or photographing. In 33 % touching short of penetration was alleged and in 21 % penetration of an orifice by an object was alleged. (2 % could not be classified under these headings). Thus over half the allegations involved some form of exploitative physical contact with the child.

Examples

Girl (7) was brought to hospital with a bleeding vagina. The story given was that she had slipped while trying to reach toys on top of a cupboard and hurt herself. Medical examination confirmed sexual abuse and parents were arrested (case 437: penetrative abuse).

Girl (14) referred by child health consultant because her 'sexualised behaviour' (staying out late etc) suggested to him she might be showing effects of abuse. No supporting evidence found (case 368: behaviour change only).

Again there were marked differences between authorities: the proportion of referrals involving some form of alleged physical contact varied from 64 % in IL 3 to 31 % in C 2. However, there was no consistent pattern discriminating high from low registration rate authorities.

Suspected Perpetrators of Physical and Sexual Abuse

Overall, 89 % of suspected perpetrators of **physical injury** (whose identity was stated) were parents or parent-substitutes, ranging from 97 % in OL 1 to 77 % in IL 4. Father figures were more often involved than mother figures (46 % v 38 %). Natural fathers were more often involved than were stepfathers or cohabitees in reconstituted families. Approximately 6 % of suspected perpetrators of physical injury were relatives other than parent figures, and the remainder were non-relatives. In IL 4 the proportions of other and non-relatives were highest (13 % and 10 %). 53 % of alleged perpetrators were male and only 3 % were under 18. In 99 % of cases the child knew the alleged perpetrator, and in 90 % of cases they were living in the same household.

Mother figures were very seldom alleged to be perpetrators of **sexual abuse** – in some 2 % of cases jointly with father and 2 % alone. Father figures were alleged to be involved in some 36 % of cases and other relatives in nearly 20 %. Natural fathers were rather more often implicated than were stepfathers. In marked contrast to physical injury, some 40 % of alleged perpetrators of sexual abuse were not related to the child. However, OL 2 stood out as having only 9 % in this category, probably due to a policy decision on who should investigate so called 'stranger' abuse. 91 % of alleged perpetrators were male, 18 % were under 16, and nearly a quarter were under 18. There was a marked difference by authority in the age of alleged perpetrators of sexual abuse, with the proportion under 16 ranging from 6 % in OL 2 to 33 % in C 2. Although a comparatively high proportion of all the alleged perpetrators were unrelated to the child, they were known to their victims in 99 % of cases and lived with them in 43 %. In general, therefore, physical injury appeared to be more of a family phenomenon than did sexual abuse, but in both cases 'stranger' abuse was extremely rare.

Age and Sex of Notified Children

Table 3v shows the mean ages and the sex distribution for the main reasons for notification. Girls were identified at older ages than boys. They were nearly twice as likely to be identified for sexual abuse but less likely to be identified for physical abuse or neglect. There was a trend in the authorities with higher registration rates for children to be older and more often to be girls. The explanation probably lies in the higher proportions in those authorities who were identified for sexual abuse.

Table 3v. Age and Sex of Children Notified for Selected Reasons

Reason	Boys	Girls	Ratio F:M
	Mean Age		
Neglect	5.1	5.4	0.85:1
Physical	5.6	7.1	0.77:1
Sexual	7.4	8.0	1.85:1

Figure 1 illustrates the contrasting age distributions for boys and girls notified for neglect or safety issues, physical and sexual abuse. For boys and (though to a lesser extent) for girls there was a steep decline in age of referral for neglect and physical abuse from the peak (age 0–4). For sexual abuse the age peak in referrals for both sexes was 5–9, and at every age girls outnumbered boys.

Fig 3.i
Referred Children by Age and Sex

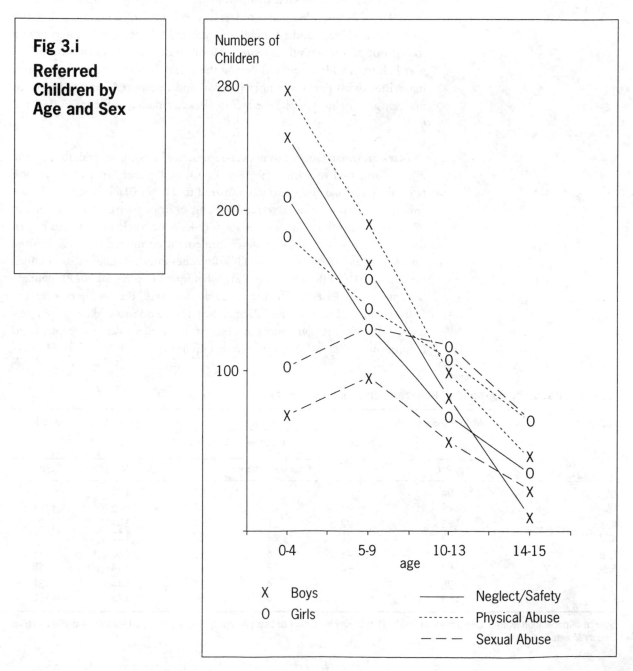

Racial Background of Referred Families

Social workers did not always give details of the racial background of the child and his or her parents. The available data are shown in table 3vi. Too much weight should not be given to the figures themselves because of the problem of missing data, but the relative proportions of white versus black and asian may be compared with population figures for 'whites' taken from the 1991 Census. The rank order is very similar, suggesting that the proportions of black and asian children referred for investigation may not be too far out of line with their representation in the local populations. In IL 4 over half the children referred during the research period were from ethnic minorities, with the other inner London and one outer London boroughs not being far behind, while the picture was completely different in IL 1 and C 2.

Black and asian families were over-represented among referrals for physical injury compared to whites (58 % v 42 %), and under-represented among referrals for sexual abuse (20 % compared to 31 %). Black african and asian families were more often referred for using an implement, such as a cane, to inflict physical injury: 40 % of asians and 43 % of black africans had beaten their children with a stick or other implement compared to 30 % of afro-caribbeans and 16 % of whites. This illustrates cultural differences in child-rearing, and the difficulty of deciding what forms of physical punishment are 'acceptable' in Britain. On the research measures, the *consequences* of the injuries inflicted on black and asian children were no more likely to be long-lasting; it was the *form* the punishment took that was unacceptable to community agents who referred these children.

Table 3vi. **Racial Background of Referred Families by Authority**

Authority	'White' Population	Referrals:			Base N.	Missing
		Black/Asian	Mixed/Other	White		
	% Pop.	% families referred			No.	No.
OL 1	94	3	4	93	129	11
OL 2	74	39	7	54	74	41
IL 1	82	22	21	57	104	21
IL 2	79	21	20	59	123	15
IL 3	76	41	4	55	160	31
IL 4	64	46	12	42	144	48
C 1	96	7	4	89	544	132
C 2	99	1	3	96	149	162

Source of population figures: Department of Health (1990) Key Indicators of Local Authority Social Services 1988/89 and 1991 Census County Monitors

Example

The police brought a seven year old child to casualty on a police Place of Safety order: she had run away after a beating from her mother for stealing a packet of crisps. The child was regularly beaten as a punishment by her mother while her aunts held her down. No serious injuries were found.

Sources of Referrals

The most common sources of referral were teachers, school nurses and education welfare staff (23 %). Health staff (health visitors, hospitals, general practitioners etc) and lay people (household members, other relatives, friends, neighbours or the child himself) each contributed approximately 17 %. Other sections of the social services department contributed 13 %, followed by police or probation (12 %). Only 6 % of the referrals were anonymous. A mixture of other sources, including nurseries and voluntary bodies, contributed the remainder. The different referral sources tended to specialise to a significant extent in the type of maltreatment that they reported. Police and probation were most likely to report sexual abuse; health sources were most likely to report physical injury; anonymous sources were particularly likely to make allegations of neglect. There were highly significant differences between authorities in sources of referral. For example, lay sources were five times as common in C 2 as they were in IL 4 (25 % v 5 %); while education sources were over twice as common in IL 1 as they were in OL 1. High registration rate authorities were not distinguished by any particular pattern of sources.

In summary, there were wide variations in the type and seriousness of alleged maltreatment investigated in the eight sample authorities, in the age, sex and racial background of the children and in the sources who referred them. Some authorities had a lower threshold for child protection investigations than others but they were not always the ones with higher rates or children on the register. Similarly, the four authorities with high rates of children on the register did not all have more children referred for investigation. There was, however, a consistent trend for high-register-rate authorities to have more children referred for sexual abuse investigations.

Chapter 4

Characteristics of Referred Families

We have seen that neither the numbers of children entering the system nor their characteristics distinguished in a straight-forward way between the paired authorities: those with high rates of children on the register did not necessarily have higher referral rates or more serious cases. This chapter will examine differences in the family backgrounds of the children referred in the eight authorities.

Types of Household

Family size and features of family composition are illustrated in Table 4i. Overall, only 30 % of the families were headed by the two 'original' parents. The NSPCC survey found that less than half the children *registered* for physical or sexual abuse or neglect between 1983–87 were living with both natural parents, a similar proportion to that found here for *referred* children (Creighton & Noyes, 1989). In OL 1 (the bottom of the range) 34 % of investigated families were headed by a lone parent while the highest proportion was found in IL 2 – 48 % The proportion in reconstituted families ranged from 9 % in IL 4 to 29 % in C 1. It is notable that the structure of families investigated in more prosperous and stable areas – the counties and outer London boroughs – appeared quite similar to that of families investigated in inner city areas. Even in OL 2 only 37 % of families were headed by both natural parents.

Table 4i. **Referred Children's Households**

Authority	No. of Children	Lone Parent	Reconstituted	Joint Parents
	Mean	%	%	%
OL 1	2.1	34	21	33
OL 2	2.1	37	20	37
IL 1	2.1	38	17	30
IL 2	2.0	48	11	33
IL 3	2.5	46	21	25
IL 4	2.7	44	9	35
C 1	2.4	37	29	29
C 2	2.1	43	22	30
ALL	2.3	36	22	30

Base N. of families: 1,825. Missing data on 63 families

Note: Other household compositions not illustrated.

Table 4ii. **Poverty Indicators among Referred Families**

Authority	Unemployment		Income Support	Temp. Acom	Material Stress Factors
	%		%	%	Mean
OL 1	50	(8.3)	45	18	0.8
OL 2	47	(7.4)	38	13.5	0.5
IL 1	69	(13.2)	61	18	1.1
IL 2	57	(11.3)	52	26.5	1.1
IL 3	50	(18.3)	46	3	1.1
IL 4	73	(21.8)	69	6	0.9
C 1	53	(10.5)	53	4.5	0.9
C 2	63	(8.0)	59	13	1.0
ALL	57		54	11	0.9
BASE N.	1206		1185	1458	1771
MISSING	682		703	430	117

% economically active local male pop. unemployed in brackets. Source: Census 1991 County Monitors

Poverty Indicators

The indicators used as indirect measures of poverty in the referred families were the lack of a wage-earner, dependence on income support, living in temporary accommodation and the social worker's mention of any of four 'material stress factors': debts, other financial problems, overcrowding or inadequate housing. Unfortunately investigating social workers did not routinely note details of the families' material circumstances and there were large gaps. Table 4ii summaries the available data. Altogether, of cases where data were available, 57 % lacked a wage-earner, 54 % were dependent on income support, 11 % were in temporary accommodation and the mean material stress factors noted by social workers were 0.9. Unemployment rates among the referred families, on the basis of these limited data, were very high compared to local male unemployment rates: in IL 4, a particularly deprived area, nearly three-quarters of referred families lacked a wage earner compared to an unemployment rate of 22 % among the economically active local male population. Between 38 % and 69 % of families in the eight authorities were dependent on income support. The proportion in temporary accommodation ranged from 3 % in IL 3 to 26 % in IL 2. The mean material stress factors recorded by social workers ranged from 0.5 in OL 2 to 1.1 in three of the inner London boroughs.

The overall picture was of deprived families living in poverty. Although OL 2 stood out as having fewer deprived families, in general there was no tendency for the authorities with lower registration rates to be investigating significantly more or less prosperous referrals. In all areas families referred because of suspected sexual or emotional abuse were in significantly less deprived circumstances than those referred with allegations of neglect or physical injury.

Parent Factors

The records were checked for the five years before the index referral, or from the case opening if this was less than five years, and information recorded about the following 'deviant' parental characteristics was abstracted: either parent (or parent figure) found guilty of a criminal offence; either parent (or parent figure) treated for a mental illness, including a suicide attempt; either parent (or parent figure) abused drugs or alcohol; either parent abused as a child; violence by one parent on another. It must be re-emphasised that these characteristics were not chosen because they are established causes of child maltreatment, but because there is evidence from the literature that they *may* be implicated as risk factors. Table 4iii shows the proportion of cases in the eight sample authorities where these parent characteristics were recorded. Criminal records were recorded in 13 %, mental illness in 13 %, substance abuse in 20 %, a parent abused in childhood in 12.5 % and violence to a partner in 27 %.

There were highly significant differences between authorities in the proportions of children referred whose parent figures had criminal records, had been treated for mental illness, abused substances and used violence on a partner. There were no differences in whether a parent had been abused as a child. The authorities with high rates of children on the register did not show consistently higher or lower levels of deviant characteristics among the parents of children referred for investigation.

Table 4iii. **Problems of Parent Figures**

Authority	Crim. Record	Ment. Ill	Subst. Abuse	Abus. as Child	Partner Violence
	% of families investigated				
OL 1	27	25	21.5	13	30
OL 2	7	18	19	11	27.5
IL 1	27.5	15	31	11	30
IL 2	22	20	22	13	23
IL 3	19	9	13	13	23
IL 4	9	9	17	8	17
C 1	10	10	15	12.5	28
C 2	15	15	30.5	15	29
ALL	13	13	20	12.5	27
BASE N.	1771	1771	1774	1767	1777
MISSING	117	117	114	121	111

Table 4iv. **Previous Suspected Maltreatment and Care Orders**

Authority	Previous CP Investign	Previously On CPR	Previous Care Order
	% referred families		
OL 1	43	14	7
OL 2	30	13	5
IL 1	49	15	16
IL 2	39	16	12
IL 3	49	18	15
IL 4	33	15	10.5
C 1	49.5	17	9
C 2	46	10.5	8
ALL	45	15	10
BASE N.	1782	1777	1804
MISSING	106	111	84

Previous Contact with Social Services

Only 35 % of the families referred for investigation were new to social services: 65 % had previously been in contact. The 8 authorities varied significantly around this average, from 26 % being first referrals in IL 1, to 45 % in IL 4. In the 4 authorities with lower rates of children on the register the proportions of first referrals were consistently higher. Of those already known to social services, 21 % were cases already open to a social worker – of whom 10 % were actually on the child protection register.

Previous contact in itself should not be associated with risk of child maltreatment. However, previous investigation for suspected maltreatment and previous care orders are more probable indicators of increased current risk. Table 4iv shows the proportion of children (index children or their siblings) who had experienced these events.

With 45 % of all the referred families having been previously investigated after allegations of child maltreatment, 15 % of children or their siblings having been on the child protection register and 10 % having been the subject of Care Orders, child abuse and neglect often appeared to be a chronic phenomenon. In general, referrals in authorities with high rates of children on the register showed higher levels of previous maltreatment and compulsory legal intervention.

In summary, the families referred on suspicion of abuse or neglect in one authority were not the same as those referred in another. They differed in household characteristics, in levels of parental deviance and in previous history. Although the data were inadequate, there were also clear differences in poverty and material stress in different authorities. Most of these differences appeared to be related to population characteristics of the authorities. Thus most of the differences in characteristics of families at the point of referral did not appear to play any part in explaining differences between paired authorities in the rate of children placed on the register. However, there were some systematic differences between the high and low registration rate authorities: children entering the child protection system in high rate authorities were less often first referrals – not previously known to social services; and they had experienced more previous child protection investigations and more compulsory legal intervention.

Chapter 5

The Question of Substantiation

So far we have treated the reported concerns about child maltreatment (the referrals) as non-problematic: as if a reported concern about maltreatment was the same as a 'case' of maltreatment. Before describing the way in which referred children were handled in the eight sample authorities, we must confront the difficult problem of the 'truth' or 'falsity' of these reported concerns. This issue has largely been left to parent self-help groups in this country, but it has attracted more research attention in the United States.

Besharov (1985) has pointed out that while some cases of child maltreatment are clear-cut, the majority of reports are ambiguous and fall into a grey area, and in chapter three in this report we saw how comparatively few allegations involved 'serious' physical injury where a clear decision about abuse could easily be made. Besharov argued that because legal standards and definitions are vague and over-inclusive decision-makers often have to fall back on value judgements and personal interpretations. Social workers are the main gatekeepers of the child protection system, but they have no infallible methods of determining abuse or risk. Besharov (1991) has argued that more specific guidelines could improve gatekeeping.

Allegations of child maltreatment may not be substantiated for several reasons. The allegation may be the result of a misunderstanding or misperception, or of a faulty medical diagnosis. It may be impossible to gather enough supporting evidence to confirm an allegation that is denied by the suspected perpetrator, especially if there is no confirmation from the alleged victim. The allegation may be deliberately false, made out of spite or for interested motives. Robin (1991) has reviewed studies of false allegations, most of child sexual abuse. The largest concerned 576 reports to Denver social services. 47 % of these reports were not substantiated, most often because of insufficient evidence or alternative explanations. Only 8 % of the unsubstantiated reports were "fictitious" – deliberate falsifications, misperceptions and confused interpretations of situations. In general false allegations of sexual abuse were more likely to be made by adults than children, often by parents with emotional disturbance. A context of divorce and custody disputes appeared to increase the likelihood of false allegations, but most false allegations were not made maliciously. Giovannoni (1989) has examined the problem of unsubstantiated reports in a large study of child protection workers, concluding that 'screening out' certain types of allegations (for example, those made during custody disputes) without further investigation would be undesirable.

A particular problem in differentiating between substantiated and unsubstantiated reports in the present study was that in none of the eight sample authorities was it policy routinely to record the outcome of investigations. Considering the trauma that such investigations can cause this does not seem to be good practice. Besharov (1991) recommends that the categories of reasons for closing a case after an initial investigation should be standardised and the category "unsubstantiated" should be divided into two:

- Unsubstantiated, no further action
- Unsubstantiated, further services provided or arranged.

In the absence of agency categorisations, in order to assess the degree of certainty regarding abuse or neglect, research ratings had to be made, using the assessments and summaries of investigating social workers and their seniors. Seven categories were distinguished:

- Untrue/wrong allegation
- Alternative explanation accepted
- Some evidence but doubtful
- Definite evidence of abuse/neglect
- Insufficient evidence to substantiate allegation
- Risk only, no actual incident
- Other

These ratings were made on the basis of the written records which no doubt varied in the way assessments were made and recorded. The results must be interpreted cautiously. Table 5i shows that the proportion of unsubstantiated allegations (untrue, alternative explanations and insufficient evidence) stood at 49 % – very similar to the proportion reported above in the Denver study. The proportion unsubstantiated in the 8 sample authorities varied from 31 % in IL 2, to 62 % in IL 4.

There were differences in the substantiation rate of different types of abuse. Allegations of neglect were most likely to be considered untrue or wrong by social workers, and referrals for physical injury were most likely to have an alternative explanation, such as an accident or a medical cause, which the social workers accepted. Different sources of referral led to different chances of substantiation. For example, only 7 % of referrals from police or probation sources and from other social services areas were considered to be 'untrue', compared to 18 % of referrals from lay people and 44 % of anonymous referrals. A quarter of referrals from health sources were considered to have an acceptable alternative explanation, compared with 2 % from police or probation sources.

Substantiation was also influenced by whether the child her or himself told anyone about the maltreatment. Children's confirmation or otherwise was usually recorded by investigating social workers. Children referred for sexual

Table 5i. **Reasons for Not Substantiating Allegations of Abuse and Neglect**

Main Reason Referred	Untrue	Altern. Explan.	Insufft. Evidence	Total Unsubstant.
		% referred families		
Neglect	25	1	27	53
Physical Injury	12	25	16.5	53.5
Sexual Abuse	12	2	28.5	42.5
Emotional Abuse	8.5	3	41	52.5
Other	8.5	3	13	24.5
ALL	14	12	23	49

BASE N. 1,843. Missing data on 45 cases

abuse and physical injury were quite likely to tell someone themselves, or at least confirm the allegation (48 % told about sexual abuse and 42 % told about physical abuse). 'Telling' was more likely at older ages, so children referred for neglect, who were younger, rarely told (8 %). Table 5ii shows whom the child told. Teachers were the most likely to receive a child's confidences, followed by other professionals such as police, social workers, school nurses. Parents or other relatives were much less likely to be told.

Children making or confirming allegations were not always believed. 8 % of children who told were disbelieved and in 12 % of the cases where children told an alternative explanation was accepted. However, 57 % of cases where children told were substantiated by social workers, compared to 28 % of the cases where children did not tell. Thus the child's own confirmation was the most important factor in substantiating allegations of abuse. Children were no more likely to make or confirm allegations in the context of recorded access or custody disputes, but when custody disputes were recorded social workers were significantly less likely to substantiate allegations.

Table 5ii. **People Told by Child about Maltreatment**

People	Number	%
Child Did Not Tell	1187	66
Teacher	232	13
Other Professional	169	9
Parent Figure	130	7
Friend	41	2
Other Relative	26	2
Other	25	1

BASE N. 1810 Missing data on 78

The problem of substantiating allegations of abuse and neglect deserved more attention from ACPCs, in our opinion. At the very least, the outcome of the investigation should be recorded in a consistent way. With better quality information firmer conclusions could be drawn. For example, it might be appropriate to divert some types of referral which are very difficult to substantiate away from child protection procedures at the earliest possible stage: such cases might be better defined and approached through policies developed for children 'in need'. Parents and children who are caught up in an investigation also deserve a clear account of its findings.

Chapter 6

Filtering Cases out of the Child Protection System

The child protection system might be considered as a small-meshed net, in which are caught a large number of minnows as well as a smaller number of marketable fish. The minnows have to be discarded but no rules exist about the correct size of the mesh. Each fishing fleet may therefore set its own. The 'meshes' are the organisational filters operated by local child protection systems. A child who enters the system must pass through a number of organisational 'filters' before his or her name is placed on a child protection register. First, there is an unknown number of 'cases' in the community, some of whom are identified by lay people and community agents and brought to the attention of police or social services departments (referred). Following referral, some children and families will be filtered out of the system very quickly while some will be further investigated. Of these, some again will be filtered out, while the remainder go through to an inter-agency child protection conference. At this stage a further group will be filtered out of the child protection system to receive informal help or no further action, leaving a residue to be placed on the child protection register. However, we do not know much about how these filters are operated, nor how much their operation varies in different authorities (Gough et al, 1987).

Much of our current understanding of the processes at work comes from the early research carried out by Dingwall and colleagues (Dingwall et al., 1981). These researchers were interested in the manner in which cases that eventually resulted in legal action emerged from the many possible cases. They decided on an ethnographic approach to the problem, carrying out an intensive study (which included participant observation) into a small number of cases in one English county, backed up with further interviews with some professionals in 17 other areas. This approach yielded valuable insights into the roles of professionals in *identifying and confirming* child abuse and neglect. The researchers concluded that two types of evidence were used initially: the child's clinical condition and the nature of his social environment. Purely clinical settings were likely to lead to under-identification. Health visitors and social workers were in a better position to give weight also to factors in a child's environment. To help them reach decisions about what was 'deviant' as opposed to within the normal range of parenting, they were said to draw on models of "normality" in family life. Judgements of normality – especially by health visitors – were first based on the family's material environment – its "housekeeping standards". Social workers were more concerned with the family's "moral environment" – notably the quality of the relationship between the members. Since fieldworkers were very reluctant to jeopardise their continued relationship with an adult, on whose co-operation their continued surveillance of the children depended, by making open accusations of neglect or abuse, health visitors were likely to 'identify' more cases than social workers 'confirmed'.

However, in order to limit the numbers 'confirmed' to a figure that could be handled by the available resources, a third principle of selection came into play. This was "the attributing of responsibility for the deviance". Was the deviant parental behaviour knowing and intentional? Various "justifications and excuses which defeat identification" were used. These included denial by the parents, arguments that the parents were themselves victims of wider forces causing stress and deprivation and appeals to "cultural relativism". The most important "excuse" employed by agency staff was their perception that warmth and affection existed in the family in spite of the deviant behaviour. A "rule of optimism" biased social workers towards crediting parents with natural affection for their children. "Triggers" for coercive intervention were, first, the perceived presence of "parental incorrigibility" – shown by the parent who did not co-operate, allow access to the child or accept advice. However, if an appearance of co-operation was maintained, there was likely to be "an indefinite perpetuation of conditions where children may be clearly suffering from their parents' inadequacy". The second trigger for legal intervention came if knowledge about the case spilled over to a number of influential professionals in different agencies.

This important research had a great deal of influence on subsequent thinking. However, it did not offer much practical help on the issue which had emerged as so central: how to select from the mass of cases presented to the child protection system the minority where *protective* intervention, as opposed to supportive help, was necessary. Later work, especially in the United States, has taken up this issue in the form of 'risk assessment'.

Risk Assessment

Risk Assessment has been defined as a systematic decision-making process that takes place over the life of a child protection 'case'. Standard assessment instruments are used in order to provide workers with concrete and practical guidelines for determining how safe the child is, what agency resources are necessary to keep him or her safe and under what circumstances a child should be removed from home. The approach does not provide hard and fast rules, nor does it provide predictive instruments. Systematic risk assessment is intended to make decisions more visible, increase reliability between different workers or areas and improve the quality of decisions by ensuring that relevant factors are taken into account.

Meddin (1985) identified four points during the investigation when protective workers in the USA assessed risk: determining whether an emergency response was necessary; identifying the need for placement; deciding whether to involve police or take legal action. (In Britain the involvement of police is usually pre-decided by inter-agency procedures.) The criteria used to assess potential risk in these situations were as follows (in order of frequency):

- severity of the current incident
- younger age of child
- previous contact with agency over suspected abuse
- functioning of prime caretaker
- further access of perpetrator
- intent of perpetrator
- functioning of child
- cooperation of prime caretaker

These criteria were not used individually or in a formal way, but taken together they helped the workers assess the degree of risk.

Formal Risk Assessment Systems

Pecora (1991) has reviewed a number of more formal approaches in use in the United States.

The *matrix approach* uses a table of factors each of which is rated on a 3–5 point scale in terms of its contribution to 'low', 'moderate' or 'high' risk to the child. These systems have been used in the US states of Illinois, Washington and Florida to assist the decision-making of protective workers.

Empirical predictors are systems which attempt to identify a small number of factors which are believed to predict the likelihood of maltreatment. Because of the comparative rarity of serious abuse and its complicated causation, it is likely that any predictive system will produce large numbers of 'false positives' – children identified by the screening system who do not subsequently suffer abuse (Starr, 1982; Gibbons et al., 1990; Baldwin & Spencer, 1993).

Family assessment scales are behaviourally anchored scales of family functioning used to assess the level of concern for the child. The Child Welfare League of America has developed Child Well-Being Scales that assess the degree to which the child's needs are not being met – and hence, by inference, the degree of risk to the child. Thus this approach does not focus so much on the risk of maltreatment per se (Magura et al., 1987).

In Britain Waterhouse & Carnie (1992) interviewed social workers in a sample of 51 Scottish cases of sexual abuse, in order to derive more general criteria for the evaluation of risk in sex abuse cases. Social workers defined their main purpose as the determination of risk to the child, but were not using systematic methods of risk assessment. The authors classified their criteria into *primary (child care) criteria*, such as the child's age, the attitude of the alleged perpetrator and the non-abusing parent; and *secondary (disclosure) criteria serving to substantiate or refute the allegations*, such as physical signs and symptoms, whether the child confirmed the allegation, and characteristics of the parent such as substance abuse.

Thus in Britain, research has mainly concentrated on studying the professionals concerned with making the determination of risk. The present research presented an opportunity to examine characteristics of a large number of children and families entering the child protection system in different authorities. Instead of asking professionals what factors they believed to be important, or observing their behaviour in a small number of cases, we wanted to describe features which empirically distinguished between children who were filtered out of the child protection system and those who were retained within it and placed on a register.

We saw the operation of the child protection system as a dynamic process: from the large number of possible 'cases' entering the system at referral, a much smaller number had to be selected to receive inter-agency protection. This process happened over a period of time and different people might be involved in the decisions at different stages. This chapter will describe referred cases who were filtered out of the system without ever becoming the subjects of an inter-agency child protection conference.

The First Filter: No Investigation Undertaken

The first point at which referred children might be removed from the child protection systems of the eight authorities came early on. Duty staff might

Table 6i. **Decision not to Undertake Child Protection Investigation**

Authority	Number of Families	% Not Investigated	
OL 1	140	22	NS
OL 2	115	23	
IL 1	125	23	NS
IL 2	136	15	
IL 3	186	18	P<.01
IL 4	191	32	
C 1	644	25	P<.01
C 2	309	38	
ALL	1,846	26	

Missing data on 42 cases
chi-square test: Diffs. between authorities: 43.7 df 7 significance .0000

decide themselves, or after carrying out telephone checks with other agencies, that the child protection issues raised by the referral did not justify any further investigation and that the family would therefore not be directly approached. Altogether, just over a quarter of cases referred were filtered out of the system without further investigation. In about a quarter of these there was no record of phone checks with other agencies being carried out.

Table 6i shows that there were differences between the practice of different authorities. In two of the paired authorities the differences were not statistically significant, but in the other two pairs, the authority with lower official rates of children on the register filtered out a higher proportion of cases without face-to-face investigation.

The Second Filter: Investigations Not Proceeding to Conference

In about half of all the *referred* cases investigative interviews were carried out but the cases never reached the stage of an inter-agency case conference. On average, 68% of the cases actually *investigated* were filtered out. Within the paired authorities all four of those with lower official registration rates filtered out higher proportions of children. However, differences in three of the four pairs were not statistically significant (Table 6ii). Even in IL 3, the least selective authority, less than half the cases actually investigated reached the case conference stage.

In summary, just over a quarter of the cases referred for child protection concerns were filtered out of the system without any investigative interviews. Of those further investigated, 68% were filtered out before the conference. The average concealed significant differences between only two of the four pairs of authorities.

Table 6ii. **Decision Not to Proceed to Case Conference Investigation**

Authority	N. Investigated	% Not Conferenced	
OL 1	109	68	NS
OL 2	89	70	
IL 1	96	71	NS
IL 2	116	77	
IL 3	152	57	NS
IL 4	130	64	
C 1	484	67	P<.05
C 2	192	74.5	
ALL	1,368	68	

chi-square: conferenced v. not conferenced: 17.6 DF 7 Significance .013

Factors Associated with the Operation of the Filters

What factors characterised children who were filtered out of the child protection system before the conference? Were there systematic differences between the children who were discarded and those who were retained? We considered possible differences under five headings. First, *factors to do with the child*: age, gender, race and household type. Second, *factors to do with the abusive incident*: its type, severity, the alleged perpetrator and the source of the referral. Third, *previous history factors*: the degree of previous contact with social services, whether there had been previous legal orders and previous child protection investigations. Fourth, *factors indicative of family poverty*: whether unemployment, housing problems, dependence on income support or

Table 6iii. **Factors Associated with Operation of Filters in Child Protection System**

Factor	Cases:	
	Not investigated	Investigated No Conference
	Nature of Association	
CHILD		
Age	None	None
Gender	None	*
Race	None	None
Household	**	None
ABUSE INCIDENT		
Type	***	**
Severity	***	***
Perpetrator	***	***
Referral Source	***	***
PREVIOUS HISTORY		
Soc. Serv. Contact	***	None
Legal Orders	**	None
CR Investigations	***	**
POVERTY		
No Wage-Earner	NA[1]	None
Housing Problems	NA	None
Income Support	NA	None
Money Problems	NA	None
PARENT PROBLEMS		
Criminal Offence	NA	***
Substance Abuse	NA	**
Psych. Disorder	NA	**
Partner Violence	NA	***
Abused as Child	NA	**

Cases not investigated.
chi-square significance of association: * <0.5 ** <.01 *** <.001

money problems were mentioned in the record. Fifth, *factors indicative of parental deviance*: parent committed criminal offences, dependent on drugs or alcohol, had a psychiatric disorder, mention of parent being abused as a child and mention of violence to spouse or partner. It must be emphasised that the researchers used case records to extract this information and were therefore dependent on the quality of social work assessments.

Table 6iii summarises the associations between these factors and the operation of filters that removed children from the child protection system. Children were *more likely to be filtered out without investigation* if:

- there was no man in the household (especially not a step-father figure);
- the referral concerned neglect or emotional abuse rather than physical or sexual abuse;
- the allegations were of less serious abuse (less serious injury, no physical neglect or no physical sexual contact);
- the alleged perpetrator was not in the household;
- the source of the referral was anonymous or a lay person (and especially if the source was *not* the police);
- the family had no previous contact with social services;
- there had been no previous legal orders or investigations for suspected abuse or neglect.

Investigated cases were *more likely to be filtered out without a conference* if:

- there were only girls in the family;
- the allegations concerned neglect or emotional abuse;
- the alleged abuse or neglect was less severe;
- the perpetrator was not in the household;
- there had been no previous investigations of alleged abuse or neglect;
- no parent figure was recorded as having a criminal record, a history of substance abuse, a psychiatric disorder, a history of domestic violence or having been abused as a child.

Selecting the 'Right' Children for Conference

We have seen that in the eight sample authorities children referred because of concerns about abuse or neglect had significantly different chances of being considered at a child protection conference. A child investigated in C 2, for example, had a one in four chance of reaching the conference, while a child investigated in IL 3 had approaching a one in two chance. However, we cannot say that "too many" children were filtered out in C 2, or "too few" in IL 3. In deciding whether the filters were being operated appropriately or inappropriately in the different authorities we need criteria for selecting children who 'should' be conferenced. The problem is that while *Working Together* provides a general statement of the purpose of the child protection procedures, no detailed criteria or policies have been developed, either nationally or in any of the sample authorities, which could identify cases where these procedures should or should not be applied. A researcher therefore cannot measure cases against an agreed set of criteria determining the need for child protection procedures and plans. We nevertheless wanted to take the enquiry a little further and therefore had to construct a research criterion of 'need for protection'.

Composite Measure of Need for Protection

In devising a research standard which could be used to identify children for whom child protection procedures were appropriate, we took into account first, whether the incident which caused referral to the system had been regarded as *substantiated* by investigation; and second, whether factors had been recorded which might be associated with *future risk* to the child. *Substantiation* was determined by a research rating of the recorded opinions of the initial investigators in the two weeks following referral or before the conference, whichever was earlier (see chapter 5). The risk factors included were:

- the seriousness of the referral incident. Physical abuse referrals were taken to be more serious if other injuries as well as bruising were inflicted or the injury had consequences likely to last for more than 2 weeks. Sexual abuse was considered more serious if physical contact was alleged. Neglect was considered more serious if physical neglect was involved, not just leaving the child alone.

- For neglect and physical abuse, the child being under five and hence more physically vulnerable.

- The alleged perpetrator's being in the same household as the child.

- At least one previous investigation for abuse or neglect.

- Characteristics of a parent figure which might affect his or her capacity for parenting (substance abuse, psychiatric illness, criminal record, violence to partner).

We recognise that these factors are not proven 'risk factors'. They provide a way of classifying or grouping children referred to the system. For the purposes of this research a substantiated case with many of the listed factors indicating future risk had more need of protection than an unsubstantiated case with few risk factors.

Table 6iv. **Physical Abuse: Effect of Substantiation and Risk on Decision to Conference**

Substantiated	Number of Risk Indicators		
	0.2 (394)	3+ (398)	All (802)
	% Reaching Case Conference		
Yes (380)	46	56.5	52
No (422)	4	7	5
All (802)	21	34	27.5
Missing date on 37 cases			

Physical Abuse: Need for Protection

Table 6iv shows the effect of the allegation being substantiated and of the number of risk factors on the decision to conference cases of physical abuse. Unsubstantiated cases were very unlikely to reach the conference no matter what the level of risk. Within substantiated cases, those with higher (measured) risk were rather more likely to reach the conference (56.5% v 46%).

A possible indication of 'missed' cases of physical abuse – that should have been conferenced but were not – is the number of substantiated cases in the highest risk category that did not reach conference. Fifty-six (41%) of the 137 substantiated referrals for physical abuse with four or more indicators of risk were not considered at a child protection conference. In 20 of these cases legal or other action was taken to protect the child, without referring the matter to an initial conference. However, this still left 36 referrals (26% of all substantiated cases of physical abuse in the highest risk category) leading neither to an initial conference nor to any recorded protective intervention, nor to other supportive help. Referrals from lay sources were particularly likely to drop out in this way.

Examples

A seven year old boy living in overcrowded, poor conditions with mother and her cohabitee (a man with criminal convictions who had assaulted her) and two younger siblings was referred by teacher because of a bruised eye he claimed was caused by a punch from mother. There had been many previous investigations and all the children had previously been on the register. An older child had been seriously injured and placed for adoption. The referred child had a learning disability. SW visited but accepted mother's explanation of an accident, even though the paediatrician advised that the nature of the injury was not consistent with the explanation. The police insisted on a strategy meeting where the social services decided to take no further action (case 894).

Child aged four living with mother and her cohabitee told father on an access visit that mother's boyfriend hit him hard and made him sit in cold water because he wet the bed. The child had complained before. This time he 'became hysterical' when it was time to go home. Both father and boy-friend had criminal convictions and there was a history of domestic violence. There had been previous child protection investigations. The social worker visited and recorded that there were no concerns about mother's ability to care adequately (case 122).

Neighbour called police when he found that father had hit child aged 13 twice in the face causing him to fall and cut open his head. This had happened after child came in late. There had been a previous child protection investigation and there were suspicions of drug abuse by the parents. A social work investigation was started but although child protection procedures were alluded to no decision was ever made on whether they would be invoked (case 1323).

Nursery referred a two-year old child who had burn marks on his fingers and red marks round his neck. When the duty social worker visited, mother was unable to give an explanation. There had been nine previous allegations of injuries to the child, who had previously been on the register. After a medical and discussion with a senior it was concluded that the marks were 'indicative of lack of supervision and possible rough handling' and needed no further action. Following this, the child continued to be referred for minor injuries and there were also allegations that a Schedule 1 offender was in the house. Mother was warned but no other action taken (case 1158).

It would be equally inappropriate to conference unnecessarily many unsubstantiated, low-risk cases. Only 10 cases in total fell into this category. Thus it appeared that cases of physical abuse were more likely to be 'missed' by the procedures than included in them unnecessarily.

Sexual Abuse: Need for Protection

Compared with physical abuse, higher-risk cases of sexual abuse were a little more likely to reach the conference stage, and the level of risk appeared to influence the decision to conference even when the case was not substantiated (Table 6v). Within substantiated cases, 36% of low risk cases were conferenced compared to 60% of high-risk ones.

Of 49 substantiated referrals for sexual abuse in the highest risk category, only 13 never reached an initial child protection conference and seven of these received legal or other forms of protection. Thus very few serious cases of sexual abuse had their needs for protection overlooked. Of the six who did, five were county referrals: in London there was only one apparently 'missed' high risk case of sexual abuse in the whole sample.

Table 6v. **Sexual Abuse: Effect of Substantiation and Risk on Decision to Conference**

| Substantiated | Number of Risk Indicators | | |
	0–2 (296)	3+ (178)	All (474)
	% Reaching Case Conference		
Yes (272)	36	60	46
No (202)	4	21	9
All (474)	21	45	30
Missing date on 47 cases			

Example

A seven year old boy was referred from school because he was said to be 'simulating the sex act' – feeling other boys, pulling their trousers down etc. He talked about having been touched by another relative when he had lived in a previous area. At the same time aunt alleged that child watched pornographic videos at home and called 'sex lines'. There were ten previous referrals for abuse and neglect. Father had a criminal record and used violence on mother. Nothing much seemed to be done in response to this latest referral at a time when the office was under great pressure (case 2066).

Only five low-risk, unsubstantiated cases (4%) reached an initial conference. As with physical abuse, there is little evidence that sexual abuse cases at low risk were unnecessarily conferenced.

Neglect: Need for Protection

In comparison with physical and sexual abuse, referrals for neglect were much less likely to reach the conference stage at every level of substantiation

Table 6vi. **Neglect: Effect of Substantiation and Risk on Decision to Conference**

| Substantiated | Number of Risk Indicators | | |
	0–2 (173)	3+ (195)	All (368)
	% Reaching Case Conference		
Yes (175)	9	41	28.5
No (193)	1	1	1
All (368)	4	23	14
Missing date on 24 cases			

and risk. Of the 66 substantiated referrals in the highest risk category, 36 (54%) were not conferenced. Although 12 of these received protection by other means, by-passing the conference, that left 24 (36%) apparently 'missed'.

Examples

A one year old baby and 7 year old sibling living with mother and boy-friend in a squat were referred by the hospital after mother had been admitted with a knife wound inflicted by boyfriend. There was concern about the safety of the children left with this violent man who had stated he would not look after them. However, it was decided that this was a housing not a child protection issue. The case was referred to the health visitor while a student social worker tried to look into the housing problems (case 318).

Child aged three was referred by day nursery for concerns about inadequate clothing and nits and soon afterwards the family was also referred as a result of a hospital Accident and Emergency Department audit, which had brought to light three recent unexplained injuries to the oldest child which had been considered accidental. There had been a number of earlier investigations and the children had previously been on the register. The parents abused drugs and alcohol and there were many other problems. The family moved away during the investigation, but it was decided that information could not be passed to the new area without the parents' permission, as the children's names were no longer on the register. A little while later information came that the oldest child had drowned apparently accidentally at the family's new home (case 814).

Grandmother and neighbours reported concerns for a one year old living with mother and cohabitee who abused drugs and alcohol. There was screaming and shouting late at night. When grandmother visited that evening she found mother apparently passed out on the sofa and the cohabitee who was drunk and aggressive refused her admittance. The police and emergency duty social worker broke in after they could see the baby lying on the floor and could get no response from the adults. It was decided there was not enough risk to remove the baby. At this time mother said that her cohabitee wanted to photograph the baby naked and she felt his family enjoyed blue movies and porn. There continued to be alarms over the next few days and the police broke into the flat again. The social workers then went on strike and no further action was recorded (case 284).

Only one low-risk, unsubstantiated case of neglect reached the conference.

In summary, there was very little sign in any of the sample authorities that unsubstantiated cases with few 'risk' indicators were being considered by the child protection conference. However, a significant minority or substantiated cases with many indicators of risk did *not* reach the conference stage.

Differences Between Authorities in Selection of High Risk Cases

Altogether, 33% of substantiated, lower-risk referrals reached an initial conference compared to 53% of substantiated, higher-risk referrals – a highly significant difference. There were some differences between authorities in the extent to which they were targeting the higher risk cases (on our measures) for conference (Table 6vii). IL 4, for example, conferenced nearly three-quarters of substantiated cases with three or more risk indicators, but under a fifth of lower-risk ones, while C 1 conferenced only 56% of high-risk cases but as many as 41% of low-risk ones. The differences in practice between the paired authorities, however, once levels of risk and substantiation were controlled, did not reach statistically significant levels. Some authorities, such as IL 2 and C 2, were apparently setting a particularly high threshold for invoking full child protection procedures. Further specific evaluative research would be needed to find out whether setting a high threshold had any harmful consequences – whether, for example, excluded high risk cases went on to receive further, more serious abuse – or whether, on the contrary, the policy spared children and families the unnecessary stress of the conference as well as saving professional time and resources.

Table 6vii. **Selection of Substantiated Cases for Conference in 8 Authorities**

Authority	Investigated Cases that were Substantiated	
	Risk Level	
	0–2 (442)	3+ (465)
	% Conferenced	
OL 1 (79)	24	52
OL 2 (61)	36	54
IL 1 (55)	24	57
IL 2 (90)	18	35
IL 3 (123)	40	65.5
IL 4 (67)	26	76
C 1 (308	41	56
C 2 (124)	26	42
ALL (907)	33	53***
Missing date on 33 cases		

*** P<.001
chi square (conferenced v. non-conferenced, high risk cases) 19.6 df 7 sig .006

The Child Protection Investigation

We studied the process of the investigation itself under the following headings:

- the number and status of people who influenced decisions before the case conference and whether there was disagreement between them;

- the organisation of the investigation: whether the case was allocated; whether inter-agency strategy meetings were held to plan the approach; how many interviews were held, with whom; the use of medical examinations.

Cases who were filtered out without any further investigation were excluded from this analysis.

People Influencing the Decision

Fewest people were involved in decisions about neglect cases and most in sexual abuse cases. Police were especially likely to be involved in sexual abuse decisions (48%), while other professionals such as teachers and health visitors were more likely to influence decisions about physical and emotional abuse. Relatives were seldom involved in decisions about the investigation (4.6%). Disagreement between decision-makers was rarely recorded (3% of cases investigated). Social work managers (such as duty seniors or team leaders) were the key people in making decisions about how the investigation should be handled in all the authorities. Investigated cases were more likely to go through to conference if:

- more people were recorded as influencing the decision-making (mean 2.66 v. 2.28);

- social work managers (not just social workers) were involved (mean 1.4 v. 1.1);

- child protection advisers were involved (mean .12 v. .07);

- police officers were involved (mean .33 v. .15). The involvement of police officers in decision-making remained highly significant, even when the level of risk was controlled.

The involvement of other professionals in decision-making was not a significant influence.

Organisation of the Investigation

In less than half the cases was a social worker allocated to co-ordinate the investigation. When one was allocated, the case was more likely to reach the

Table 6viii. **Action Taken Against Alleged Perpetrators**

Perpetrator	Physical Abuse (820)	Sexual Abuse (499)
	% Referrals	
Removed from Household	4.5	13
Charged/Cautioned	4	16

conference whether the referral was for neglect (58% v. 41%), physical abuse (63% v. 38%) or sexual abuse (71% v. 42%).

If an inter-agency meeting (a strategy meeting) was called to plan the investigation, cases of neglect were more likely to reach the conference (19% of those conferenced had a strategy meeting versus 5% of those investigated but not conferenced). Strategy meetings had no such effect in cases of physical abuse (9% v. 7%) or sexual abuse (25% v. 31%). Strategy meetings in any case were rare outside the London boroughs.

Medical examinations were held in 11% of neglect investigations, 51% of physical abuse investigations and 27% of sexual abuse investigations. Cases that reached the conference were significantly more likely to receive medical examinations and had significantly more investigative interviews (4.2 v. 2.1). Cases investigated for sexual abuse had most interviews and those investigated for neglect fewest. Thus, in general, cases that reached the conference appeared to be the ones that were more thoroughly investigated – more often allocated, with more interviews and medical examinations – but it must be remembered that these cases were also the most serious.

Protective Acts

So far we have described which investigations produced further action under the child protection system. Were there other results of these investigations? Possible results were pre-defined as *protective acts* or *other services*. We shall deal first with protective acts undertaken during the child protection investigation before the case conference. These were classified according to whether they were focussed on the perpetrator or the child. In only a small minority of cases of physical abuse was the perpetrator removed from the child's household, by compulsion or persuasion, or charged with an offence (Table 6x). A slightly larger minority of perpetrators of sexual abuse was removed from the household, charged with an offence or cautioned. Aid to remove was provided by the social services department in only one case of physical and one of sexual abuse. It is possible that more police action was taken against perpetrators than was recorded in social work records, the source of the research data. As they stand, the data show that direct action

Table 6ix. **Removal of Children from Home during Investigation**

Type of Abuse	Number	Informal	Type of Removal: Accommodation	Legal Order	All
Physical	822	53 (6)	21 (2.5)	31 (4)	105 (12.7)
Sexual	504	16 (3)	9 (2)	14 (3)	39 (7.7)
Neglect	378	12 (3)	6(1.5)	27 (7)	45 (11.9)
Emotional	59	3 (5)	1 (2)	0	4 (6.7)
Other	71	1 (1)	3 (3)	3 (3)	7 (9.8)
ALL	1,834	85 (4.6)	40 (2.1)	75 (4)	200 (10.9)

against alleged perpetrators of physical and sexual abuse was rarely taken. There was no significant variation by authority.

Protective acts directed at the child were categorised as removal from home – informally, by the social services providing accommodation or by legal order – and other protective action. Children referred for physical abuse were most likely to be removed from home during the investigation (13%, but only 4% under a legal order). Cases referred for neglect or 'other' reasons were next most likely: these were usually very young children. Children referred for sexual or emotional abuse were least likely to be removed from home during investigation (Table 6 ix). There were some significant differences in practice between the 8 authorities, with IL 3 particularly likely to resort to legal protective intervention.

Almost 90% of children, therefore, remained at home throughout the period of the child protection investigation and legal intervention to remove the child under an emergency order was very unusual, occurring in only 4% of all cases referred.

Other protective actions taken during the investigation were identified by the researchers in 164 cases (8.9%). They were most likely to be taken in cases of sexual abuse.

Thus, in the majority of cases referred for investigation (73%) no protective action was taken at all. There were differences by authority, with IL 1 and IL 2 more likely to undertake protective acts. There was also a difference in relation to the reason for referral: cases referred for sexual abuse were most likely to receive some protection and cases referred for emotional abuse and neglect least likely.

We recorded whether, during the period of investigation or at its close, other services – of a supportive rather than primarily protective nature – were provided for the family. These were separated into referrals to other agencies and all other services provided by the social services department. Less than 10% of cases investigated for physical or sexual abuse or neglect received either of these services. Approximately 15% of cases investigated for emotional abuse or 'other' reasons did so. There was significant variation by authority, with some of the London authorities offering more help to families.

If, during or immediately following the close of the investigation, no protective action was taken, no services were offered and the case did not proceed to conference, the case was regarded as having *no results*. 44% of all the investigated cases fell into this category. These were cases who had an average of 2 investigative interviews which produced no outcome – no interagency conference, no protective intervention and no family support services. Table 6x shows the variation by authority.

Table 6x. **Referrals Where Investigation Led to No Service or Protection**

Authority	Investigated Cases	
	Some Protection/Service	No Protection/Service
OL 1	67 (61.5)	42 (38.5)
OL 2	53 (60)	36 (40)
IL 1	71 (74)	25 (26)
IL 2	58 (50)	58 (50)
IL 3	93 (61)	59 (39)
IL 4	81 (62)	49 (38)
C 1	259 (53)	227 (47)
C 2	88 (46)	104 (54)
ALL	770 (56)	600 (44)

chi square 29.3 df 7 sig .0001 percentage in brackets

In summary, we have seen that many children and families were sucked into the child protection system to no apparent purpose. About a quarter of the referred cases were quickly filtered out without any face-to-face interviews. Of the remainder, over 40% were discarded from the system with no apparent need for any protective intervention and no offer of other services.

Children were rarely considered at a case conference unless there were clear indicators of risk and substantiated incidents of neglect and abuse, but a substantial minority of children *with* these indicators were not taken to a case conference. Referrals for neglect were most likely to be filtered out before the conference stage. In some of the eight sample authorities there was clearer targeting of high risk cases and thresholds for invoking child protection procedures appeared to be set at a higher level than was the case in others.

It seems undesirable for two reasons that so many children were drawn into the system apparently unnecessarily. First, the burden of 'unproductive' work represented a waste of the scarce resource of social workers' time. Second, too many families were exposed unnecessarily to investigative interviews and might have been left reluctant to approach social services for help they really needed. Investigations of alleged neglect were especially likely to be unproductive, and yet these often concerned families struggling in the most difficult circumstances.

Chapter 7

The Initial Protection Conference and its Decisions

We have seen that, of the 1,888 cases referred because of child protection concerns, 443 (23.5%) reached an initial inter-agency child protection (CP) conference. This chapter will describe the conferences and their decisions.

Time Taken to Convene a Conference

Working Together (5.15.3) recommends that initial CP conferences should normally be held within eight working days of referral with a maximum gap of 15 days. This may often be difficult to achieve in practice if appropriate inter-agency representation is to be secured. The mean number of days between referral and conference in our sample (drawn from eight different authorities) was 34. Only 17% of conferences were held within eight days of referral, although if working days only had been counted the proportion would be somewhat higher.

Conference Attendance

There were differences between the authorities in policy over who should chair conferences. In the outer London authorities the chair was normally taken by one of a small number of central child protection or child-care specialists. In IL 3 and 4 and in C 2 chairing was normally the responsibility of the area-based child protection specialist advisers. In the remaining authorities, the chair was usually taken by a manager based in the same area who was not a child protection specialist.

On average, 7.4 professionals (excluding the chair) attended the conference. There was significant variation between authorities, with most attending on average in OL 2 (11.2) and fewest in IL 3 (6.4). Field social workers and senior social workers attended nearly all conferences. Child protection advisers (other than chairs) were present at nearly a quarter. Council legal representatives were present at 29% of conferences. Apart from social services staff, police officers were most often represented (82% of conferences). In London specialist police from Child Protection Teams were mostly involved, but this was not usual in the counties. Nurses (including health visitors, ward staff and nurse managers) followed with 78% attendance. Then came teachers or education-based social workers (61%). Doctors were the least represented professional grouping (39% of conferences). General practitioners rarely attended (19%). There were significant differences between authorities in the types of professional who were present at the conferences, suggesting that local policies and professional relationships were very important.

Working Together (6.14) states that in principle parents and children should be included in all conferences. We did not systematically record the attendance of children, but it was certainly most uncommon. Parents very rarely attended the whole of the conference (3%). It must be remembered that these data were collected in 1991-2, before new guidance in *Working Together* had been implemented. There was clearly a long way to go (Table 7i) but several of the authorities have subsequently revised their policies.

Content of Discussion

For 70% of the conferences, full minutes had been taken and were available. From a pre-defined list, we attempted to identify the topics which had been discussed and were regarded as important enough to figure in the minutes. The topics were:

● the abuse incident itself, extent of injuries etc

● the child's health and development, other than the actual abuse incident

● the adequacy of parenting and care given to the child

● facts and comments about the parents' past history and behaviour

● family relationships

● housing

● family finances

● sources of social support available to the family

Table 7i. **Parental Attendance at Initial Conferences**

Authority	Parent Present All/ Part of Conference
	% conferences
OL 1	77
OL 2	0
IL 1	4
IL 2	61.5
IL 3	6.5
IL 4	15
C 1	0.1
C 2	2
ALL	14
BASE N.	424
Data missing on 19 conferences	

It was striking that the family's material circumstances were not often recorded as figuring in the discussion. In only 18% of conferences were family finances mentioned as the topic of discussion (Table 7ii).

Table 7ii. **Minuted Topics of Discussion at Initial Conferences**

Topic	Minuted as Discussed
	% of conferences
Abuse Incident	94
Child's Health/Development	88
Parents' Past History	80
Family Relationships	74
Parenting/Care of Child	66
Housing	35
Social Support	26
Finances	18
BASE NUMBER	406
Data missing on 37 conferences	

Decisions Taken at the Conference

The only decisions to be taken at the initial conference are whether or not to register the child, under what category and, on registration, to allocate the key worker (*Working Together, 5.15.4*). However, the picture is not quite so simple. The conference may also decide to defer a decision, and, when new initial conferences are convened after a new incident involving a child already on the register, the conference has to decide whether that child should remain rather than be placed on the register. Table 7iii shows the decisions taken in the different authorities.

Altogether, in 51% of case conferences all or some of the children considered were placed on the register but there was significant variation by area, partly due to other differences in policy and practice. In IL 4, for example, it was policy to call new initial conferences in the case of new incidents involving children already on the register and so there was an unusually high proportion in this category. In IL 3 it appeared to be routine practice to defer taking decisions while it was unusual to defer in the other authorities. Inspection of table 7iii shows that within the paired authorities there was no consistent tendency for the higher-rate one to place more children on the register. Lower-rate authorities did tend to filter more children out of the child protection system by *not* placing them on the register but the differences were not statistically significant.

Table 7iii. **Decisions Taken at the Initial Case Conference**

| Authority | Register | | Defer | Remain |
| | No | Yes | | |
	% conferences			
OL 1 (35)	40	37	14	9
OL 2 (27)	52	37	0	11
IL 1 (28)	28	54	11	7
IL 2 (27)	26	66	4	4
IL 3 (65)	17	37	40	6
IL 4 (47)	30	32	6	32
C 1 (164)	26	64	1	9
C2 (50)	36	54	8	2
ALL (443)	29	51	10	10

Number of conferences in brackets. chi square 150.2 df 28 sig. .0000

Dissent

Conference minutes recorded formal dissent in few cases (just under 5% of conferences). However, dissent was more likely to be recorded in the conferences where decisions were deferred (just under 10%). Possibly deferred decisions are more likely when there is disagreement between conference members.

Decision on Key Worker

A key worker was named in the minutes for only 52% of the cases placed on the register. There were big differences in practice between different authorities: in C 2 90% of conferences named a key worker, compared with only 23% in OL 1. However, the fact that no key worker was named in the conference minutes did not mean that none would be allocated, as we shall see from the follow-up stage of the research. In very few cases (5% of those registered) was it explicitly stated in the minutes that a key worker could not be allocated and other arrangements would have to be made.

Reason for Referral and Conference Decision

We have seen that the reason for referral had an important effect on the chances of a case getting to conference, with cases of neglect significantly less likely to be conferenced. What was the effect on the decisions taken at the conference? Table 7iv shows that once a case reached the conference it was equally likely to be placed on the register, regardless of the reason for referral.

Table 7iv. **Reason for Referral and the Initial Case Conference Decision**

Reason for Referral	Register		Defer	Remain
	No	Yes		
		% conferences		
Neglect (52)	25	44	17	14
Physical Injury (223)	29	52	8	11
Sexual Abuse (147)	31	54	8	7
Emotional Abuse (7)	14	72	—	14
Other (14)	21	43	36	—

chi sq=25.5 df 16 sig>.10

The few cases of neglect and emotional abuse that were considered by an initial conference were treated just as seriously as were cases referred for physical or sexual abuse.

Register Categories

The categories under which cases were placed on the register are shown in table 7v. As one would expect from national statistics, there were very large differences between authorities, especially in the use of 'grave concern'. Since this category has now been abolished, there is no need to labour this point. How did the categories under which cases were registered compare with the way the problem was described at referral? Of cases originally investigated for *neglect*, 45% were registered for neglect and another 45% were registered under 'grave concern of neglect'. One case was registered as physical abuse and one as emotional abuse. Of cases originally referred as *physical injury*, 68% were registered as 'physical abuse' and 27% as 'grave concern of physical abuse'. The remainder were registered as neglect or as emotional abuse. 45%

Table 7v. **Categories Under Which Cases Were Registered**

Category	Number	%
Neglect	15	6.5
Physical Abuse	68	30
Sexual Abuse	44	19
Emotional Abuse	6	3
Grave Concern	52	23
Mixed Categories	35	15
Not Stated	8	3.5
ALL	228	100

of cases referred as *sexual abuse* were registered as such and 26% as 'grave concern of sexual abuse'. The remaining 29% were divided between the other categories. Thus the process of investigation appeared to change the way the case was perceived in a substantial minority of cases.

Were the 'Right' Cases Placed on the Register?

A composite measure of *need for protection* was described in the previous chapter and found to discriminate between cases who reached the child protection conference and those who were filtered out an earlier stage. We may now ask whether the children with more indicators of risk were more likely to be placed on the register by the child protection conference. Cases already on the register have been excluded from the analysis, which is confined to children referred for physical or sexual abuse or neglect.

Physical Abuse

The child protection conference considered 198 cases originally referred because of concerns about physical abuse. Only 18 of these were *not substantiated* during the initial investigation and of these nine were actually placed on the register, of whom seven had many risk factors. Thus only two apparently unsubstantiated, low risk cases of physical abuse were placed on the register. Of the 180 *substantiated* cases, 110 (61%) were placed on the register. Cases with three or more indicators of risk were more likely to be registered (66% v. 55%) but a substantial minority of apparently serious and substantiated cases of physical abuse were not placed on the register by the conference (25 cases, just over a third of all those substantiated with at least three risk indicators who reached the conference).

Sexual Abuse

135 cases referred because of sexual abuse were considered by conference, of whom only 16 were *not substantiated*. Eleven of these were placed on the register, of whom eight had many risk factors. Thus only three low-risk, unsubstantiated cases of sexual abuse reached the register. Of the 119 *substantiated* cases, 71 (60%) were placed on the register. 70% of sexual abuse cases with three or more risk indicators were registered by conference compared with 56% of cases with less than three indicators. Only 11 of the substantiated cases with many risk factors were not placed on the register.

Neglect

Only two of the 45 cases of neglect considered at the conference were *not substantiated* – one of these was registered. Twenty-six (60%) of the 43 substantiated cases were placed on the register. We have already seen that neglect cases in general were less likely to reach the conference: those that did so were more serious (58% were 'high risk' compared to 42% of physical and 33% of sexual abuse cases considered by conference). 73% of neglect cases with three or more risk indicators were placed on the register compared to 37% of cases with fewer than three indicators.

Patterns of Registration in Different Authorities

Comparison of the children placed on the register in different authorities was confounded by the other differences in practice between them (Table 7iii). In considering patterns of registration, cases already on the register have been excluded and deferred decisions updated by the decision taken at the reconvened initial conference – if any. We found that in five of the 42 deferred cases the conference never was re-convened.

In assessing the conference decisions in different authorities there were two dimensions to be considered: first, the *relative propensity to use registration*. If less than 60% of conferenced cases were placed on the register, an authority was considered to demonstrate a 'low propensity' to register. Authorities where 60% or more of conferenced cases were placed on the register were considered as demonstrating a 'high propensity'. The second dimension was indicated by *the degree of specificity* in the use of registration. To assess specificity we used the (admittedly arbitrary) composite measure of 'need for protection' already described in chapter 6. If an authority registered a relatively high proportion of conferenced cases with three or more risk indicators and a relatively low proportion of cases with less than three indicators, we considered that authority to be using registration in a more *specific* way. Thus, in theory, 4 patterns of registration could be distinguished:

Pattern 1: A generally high propensity to register, regardless of the measured need for protection;

Pattern 2: A high propensity to register but registration targeted more specifically at cases with greater need for protection;

Pattern 3: A low propensity to register with no differentiation according to the need for protection;

Pattern 4: A generally low propensity to register but registration targeted more specifically at cases with greater need for protection.

Table 7vi shows the percentage of conferenced cases placed on the register in the different authorities in relation to the number of risk indicators. The numbers are small, but they illustrate some differences in approaches to registration. There was no significant difference between authorities in the propensity to register cases with three or more indicators of risk: the

Table 7vi. **Conferenced Cases Placed on the Register in Different Authorities by the Need for Protection**

Authority	Need for Protection				All	
	Lower		Higher			
	N.	% Registered	N.	% Registered	N.	% Registered
OL 1	14	21	14	57	28	29
OL 2	15	33	8	62	23	43.5
IL 1	12	58	7	71	19	63
IL 2	14	71	11	64	25	68
IL 3	31	42	28	64	59	52.5
IL 4	17	41	10	70	27	52
C 1	99	67	49	82	148	72
C 2	23	52	26	58	49	55
ALL	225	55	153	69	378	60

21 cases referred for emotional abuse or 'other' reasons excluded.
Differences between areas in proportions registered:
0–2 Indicators, chi sq=19.7 df7 p.006
3+ Indicators, NS
All, chi sq 19.3 df7 p.0007

differences occurred at the lower risk levels, with conferences in some authorities being less *specific* and making more use of registration for children at apparently less risk. While conferences in most of the authorities appeared to be using the register in a fairly *specific* way – placing more of the higher risk cases on the register and fewer of the lower risk cases, C2 and IL2 were exceptions. Only three authorities – IL1, IL2 and C1 – placed over 60% of conferenced children on the register.

With the possible exception of C1 and C2, the paired authorities in the study did not show marked differences in the proportion of conferenced children who reached the register. Conferences in most of the authorities appeared to be taking the same sort of factors into account and operating in a consistent fashion.

Each possible pattern of using the register has benefits and costs. In the most commonly found pattern – relatively low propensity to register and moderate specificity – 'too many' cases who do not need protection and 'too few' who do are likely to be placed on the register. On the other hand, non-specific, high propensity to register may waste resources by registering too many cases indiscriminately. Ideally, child protection conferences would place all children with demonstrably great need for protection and only those children on the child protection register, but to achieve this the state of knowledge about 'need for protection' itself would have to improve. By developing more systematic methods of risk assessment in order to discriminate better between cases who do and do not need a protection plan, authorities could register a higher proportion of the cases at most risk. But because of the large numbers of children with at least some degree of documented risk, authorities will continue to be faced with very difficult decisions.

Chapter 8

The Pathway to Registration: An Overview

In the previous chapters we have tried to provide evidence for our view that the child protection system operates as a dynamic process, driven by decisions taken by a number of different lay and professional people at different stages. Before describing what happened to children in the period following the conference we shall stand back in order to get a better view of some of the evidence so far considered in separate chapters.

Any researcher who studies the operation of the 'ordinary' child protection services rather than special projects must be forcibly struck by the overwhelming numbers of children in need who are brought to the attention of social services because of concerns about possible abuse or neglect. In 1990 the names of some 29,600 children were added to child protection registers in England. The evidence from the eight authorities reported here suggests that at least six times as many may have been investigated but filtered out of the system (Figure 8ii). Some six out of every seven children who entered the child protection system were filtered out of it without needing to be placed on a child protection register. This represents an enormous burden of work for hard-pressed community services and also means that far too many families are left feeling 'unjustly' accused.

Differences Between Authorities

There were differences between our eight authorities in the detailed ways in which the filters were operated (Table 8i). However, significant differences in the overall proportion filtered out of the child protection system occurred

Figure 8i. **Operation of Filters in Child Protection System**

ENTRY POINT New Incident	1,888 – – – – –> 42 'Lost' Cases
1ST FILTER Checks	1,846 (100 %) – – – – – –> 478 (26 %)
2ND FILTER Further Investigation	1,368 (74 %) – – – – –> 925 (50 %)
3RD FILTER Child Protection Conference	443 (24 %) – – – – –> 128 (7 %)
RETAINED IN SYSTEM AFTER CONFERENCE	315 (16 %)
OF WHOM: ON REGISTER	272 (15 %)

**Fig 8.ii
Referrals
Reaching CPR**

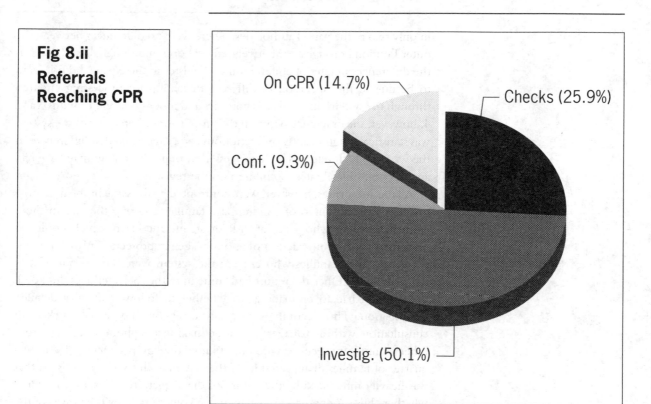

Table 8i. **Cases Filtered Out of the System at Different Stages**

Authority	First Filter	2nd Filter	3rd Filter	Total Out of CP System
		% of cases referred		
OL 1 (140)	22.1	52.9	10	85
OL 2 (115)	22.6	53.9	12.2	88.7
IL 1 (125)	23.2	54.4	6.4	84
IL 2 (136)	14.7	65.4	5.1	85.2
IL 3 (186)	18.2	46.8	5.9	70.9[1]
IL 4 (191)	31.9	43.4	7.3	82.6
C 1 (644)	24.8	50.3	7.3	82.4[2]
C 2 (309)	37.8	46.3	6.1	90.2
ALL (1846)	25.9	50.4	7.3	83.6

Missing data on 42 cases.

[1] Probability of difference between proportions exceeding zero = .006 Confidence Interval .03–.20

[2] Probability of difference between proportions exceeding zero = .0007 Confidence Interval .04–.13

in only two of the paired authorities. There were no differences between the outer London boroughs nor between inner London boroughs 1 and 2. Thus the differences in rates of children on the register in these pairs did not seem to be due to the operation of different thresholds for processing children through the system. In the paired counties and inner London boroughs 3 and 4, however, the difference between the proportions filtered out of the system was statistically significantly different from zero, suggesting that differences in the way in which referrals were processed through the system may have had an effect on official rates of children on the register.

All the authorities, however, were confronted by the same problem of how to select from the mass of children and families entering the system those comparative few who were at risk of significant harm which could be prevented by the construction of an inter-agency protection plan.

We saw how families who entered the system were filtered out of it at different stages. Once the report had come in to the social services duty desk the decision had to be made as to whether to follow it up in a detailed investigation. This decision was usually taken by duty social workers in consultation with a manager and after making telephone enquiries from other community agencies who might know the family concerned. About a quarter of families disappeared from the system at this stage, a decision that was heavily influenced by the nature of the allegation – its seriousness and whether abuse as opposed to neglect was involved – and by the power of the person who had made the referral. These families would normally know nothing about the allegation, though in a few areas it was practice to write to the parents to inform them that no further action was planned.

After investigation, another 50% of the families referred left the system. The key person in making this decision was the senior social worker or manager in charge of the duty desk. When powerful community agencies were also involved, notably the police, the family was less likely to be filtered out. The most important factor influencing the decision was whether investigation succeeded in substantiating the allegations. In about half the cases investigated the allegations were not clearly substantiated in the social work record. Other influential factors were the seriousness of the allegations and the continuing risk to the child, whether they concerned abuse or neglect, whether there had been previous similar episodes and whether the social workers perceived the parent figures as having personality character-istics that might affect adequate parenting and increase the risk of harm in the future. In selecting cases for conference social workers were not guided by any formal policies setting out the criteria to use. Nevertheless in all the authorities they seemed to be taking much the same factors into account. There was little evidence of 'too many' children who needed no protection being selected for conference and rather more evidence that a minority of children with apparently considerable needs were filtered out.

At the initial child protection conference a different set of decision-makers came into the picture, with agencies other than social services able to influence the proceedings more directly. In most authorities, at the time of the research parents very rarely attended the whole conference and did not often attend at all. Police officers were again in a position to exert strong influence since they attended the great majority of conferences. By contrast some other professional groups, notably general practitioners, seldom attended. Perhaps because of the presence of professionals from outside social services, the referrals for neglect and emotional abuse were not given lower priority at the conference as they had been at earlier stages. Although there were differences in the way the earlier filtering processes were operated, once the case reached the initial child protection conference most authorities appeared to be taking the same sort of factors into account in reaching decisions about which children should be placed on the register. Conferences in all the authorities placed around 70% of higher-risk cases on the register, although they varied more in their approach to registering lower-risk cases.

In summary, in all eight different authorities in the study most referrals were filtered out of the child protection process without being considered by an inter-agency protection conference or receiving a protection plan. The selection of children for conference and placement on the register was not random: in all authorities certain characteristics (summarised in table 8ii) made it more likely that children would be retained in the system. It appeared that characteristics of children entering the child protection system were more important than area differences in their effect on decisions to conference and register. The children who finally ended up on the child protection register were a selected group, differing in many ways from other referred children.

A number of other variables were not found to discriminate between referrals selected for conference and registration and the remainder. These were:

- Child's age group
- Child's racial background
- Unemployment of parents
- Homelessness
- Family size
- Family dependent on social security
- Financial problems recorded (other than debts)

Thus the individual poverty indicators appeared to have little influence on decision makers, though cases with many poverty indicators were more likely to be registered.

Table 8.ii. **Characteristics Associated with Selection for Conference and with Registration**

Characteristics of Cases	Selection of Children for:	
	Initial Conference	Registration
Parent Criminal Record	Yes	Yes
Reconstituted Family	Yes	Yes
Lone Parent	No	
Partner Violence	Yes	Yes
Parent Mental Illness	Yes	Yes
Previous Abuse Investigation	Yes	Yes
Parent Drug/Alcohol Abuse	Yes	Yes
Serious Allegation	Yes	
Referral for Neglect	No	No
Perpetrator in Household	Yes	Yes
Child Gender (Girl)	Yes	
Debts Recorded		Yes

In no authority were there written guidelines setting out the factors that needed to be taken into account in making decisions about children at risk. Yet it appeared that in all of them decision-makers were taking into account a combination of factors to do with the referral incident – its seriousness and type –, the continuing access of the perpetrator, the previous history and characteristics of the parents that might interfere with their ability to care for children.

Chapter 9

Six Months after Conference: The Effects of Registration

In this chapter and the next we shall describe what happened to children in the six months following their being considered at an initial child protection conference. All children not already on the register were followed up, using the minutes of the first child protection review held after the initial case conference and the social work notes covering the 26 weeks after it. Research workers extracted information from these records using standard forms. The limitations of records as data sources must again be borne in mind. In nine cases no file could be found, and in 42 cases the records were limited, often because a family had moved to another authority. Table 9i shows the composition of the follow-up sample.

144 cases were not registered by the initial conference and their status remained the same. 199 cases were registered and remained so after 26 weeks. 45 cases had changed register status, either by being removed or being added during the follow-up period. The register status of the remaining 11 cases 26 weeks after initial conference was unclear.

We evaluated the effects of registration in three ways. We asked first, whether procedures recommended in *Working Together* had been adhered to; second, what contact there had been with social workers and what services had been delivered; and third, what the outcomes had been for children and families. The detailed questions we examined were as follows.

Table 9.i. **Composition of the Follow-Up Sample**

Authority	Register Status			
	Never on CPR	Still on CPR	Other: CPR	Unclear
OL 1 (32)	15	15	2	
OL 2 (24)	14	9	1	
IL 1 (26)	11	14	1	
IL 2 (26)	8	11	6	1
IL 3 (61)	23	32	3	3
IL 4 (32)	14	12	5	1
C 1 (149)	38	87	18	6
C 2 (49)	21	19	9	
ALL (399)	144	199	45	11

Procedures

- Was a keyworker allocated continuously for the whole period?
- Was there at least one child protection review?
- Was there inter-agency representation at the review?
- Did parents attend?
- Were original plans evaluated?
- Were adequate Minutes taken?

Input of Services

- What was the pattern of social work contact with the family over the 26 weeks?
- What supportive services were arranged?
- What legal measures were used to protect children?

Outcomes

- How many children were removed from the register?
- How many children suffered repeated investigations for abuse or neglect in the 6 months after registration, and how many allegations were substantiated?
- How many were removed from home and how many were still not at home after 26 weeks?
- How many remained *safely* at home (i.e. without suffering further substantiated abuse/neglect)?

We compared the results of the eight authorities and also compared the outcomes of registered children with those who were not placed on the register. This chapter describes how far the authorities were able to adhere to recommended procedures and summarises the services provided to children and families. The next chapter considers outcomes.

Adhering to Procedures: Children on the Register

Allocation of a Keyworker

A keyworker was considered to be continuously allocated if the allocation period started before or within four weeks of the initial conference, and continued thereafter without a gap of more than two weeks – though there might have been a change of worker. Table 9ii shows that practice varied

Table 9.ii **Allocation of Keyworkers**

Authority		Allocation Period	
	None	Discontinuous	Continuous
		% cases ever on register	
OL 1 (17)	0	76.5	23.5
OL 2 (10)	0	10	90
IL 1 (15)	33	67	0
IL 2 (17)	0	12	88
IL 3 (36)	11	42	47
IL 4 (17)	6	41	53
C 1 (104)	13	27	60
C 2 (29)	0	7	93
ALL (245)	10	32	58

chi square 68.8 df 7 sig. .0000

significantly between the 8 authorities. In IL 1, where there was a prolonged social work strike, not a single case had a continuously allocated keyworker; less than a quarter did so in OL 1; while in OL 2, C 2 and IL 2 some 90% of cases were continuously allocated to a keyworker.

Holding a Child Protection Review Conference

In only 51% of cases on the register were one or more inter-agency child protection reviews held in the 26 weeks after registration. However this low average is misleading, being brought down by the low proportion of reviews (16%) called in IL 1 due to the strike, and the policy in C 1 of circulating review forms by post instead of calling review conferences. In five of the eight authorities, an inter-agency review was held in over 80% of cases. The mean number of weeks between the initial case conference and the first inter-agency review was 13.7. Again, practice varied widely: in OL 2, the reviews were held 4.3 weeks on average after initial conference, while in C 2 the gap was 16.7 weeks.

A mean 6.6 professional staff (excluding chairs) attended child protection reviews, ranging from 7.6 in C 2 to 5.4 in OL 1. The average attendance by professionals outside the social services department was 4.3, ranging from 1.9 in OL 2 to 5.4 in C 2. Table 9iii shows which professional groups were most likely to attend. As with initial conferences, the police were most often present and general practitioners and psychiatrists were rarely present. The average attendance by family members was 0.6. Authorities were developing their policies on family participation at different speeds. For example, in OL 2 no family members attended review conferences while in OL 1 a

Table 9.iii. **Professionals other than Social Services Attending Child Protection Reviews**

Professional Group	% Attendance
Police	68*
Health Visitors	48
Other Nursing	31
Nurse Managers	27*
Head Teachers	20
Other Medical	18*
Class Teachers	18
Probation Officers	17
Education Welfare	14
Other Teaching	9
General Practitioners	8
Psychiatrists	5
Base N. Conferences where attendance recorded:	125

*Statistically significant difference between practice in different authorities

family member attended three-quarters of them. On average, mothers were present for all or part of 30% of reviews, fathers 21%, children and other relatives each 4%.

The topics most often recorded as being discussed at those reviews where full minutes were kept were the degree to which family members were co-operating with the protection plan (67%), the child's behaviour and development and other family problems (65%) and the degree of risk to the child (64%). Reference was made back to the original plan in almost four-fifths, and in half the cases some or considerable progress in implementing the plan was recorded by the conference members. In 10% there was little or no progress and in 8% the original plan was rescinded. There were major differences in the way minutes were kept in the different authorities so too much weight cannot be put on this analysis. On average, full minutes were available in 60% of conferences; notes or decision sheets in 34% and less than that in 6%

In summary, therefore, there were significant differences between the eight authorities in the extent to which recommended procedures for children placed on the child protection register were adhered to. OL 2, IL 2 and C 2 were most able to implement procedures: close on 100% of children on the register had a named keyworker, who was nearly always allocated soon after the initial conference and continued without any gaps in allocation. In C 2 there was a specialised child protection service, with district co-ordinators and a specialist social work team, but this was not the case in IL 2: a

Table 9.iv. **Organisation of Social Work With Families on Register**

Authority	Supervision Mentioned	SW Plan Mentioned	Progress Summary	File Well Organised	Formal SW Methods Used
			% registered cases		
OL 1 (15)	33	13	13	67	20
OL 2 (10)	40	100	30	100	80
IL 1 (15)	27	53	0	33	7
IL 2 (18)	61	67	50	89	11
IL 3 (33)	45	58	45.5	76	3
IL 4 (16)	38	81	81	69	25
C 1 (107)	24	40	13	41	20
C 2 (27)	56	89	22	89	44

specialist system, therefore, was not necessary to safeguard resources for child protection. In these three authorities there was further evidence of generally good organisation and control of work. For example, in the majority of registered cases there were references in the record to supervision, social work plans were described and almost 90% of records were considered by the researcher to be well-organised (Table 9iv). In some other authorities, notably IL 1 and C 1, the work appeared less well structured. In general, low register rate authorities appeared to show more signs of organisation.

Structured social work methods (such as family therapy or formal counselling) were not often used even in well organised authorities.

Input of Services

Social Work Contact with Family Members

The researchers counted every face-to-face contact between a social worker and a family member (index child, mother or father figure, other adult family member) that was noted in the social work record during the 26 weeks after the initial conference. Contacts involved a mother figure in 74% of cases and a father figure in 31%. Eleven per cent of all the contacts were with a child on his or her own.

For the total follow-up sample there was a mean 9.9 contacts, but the child's register status made a marked difference. The pattern over the six months following the initial protection conference is illustrated in Figure 9i, showing that cases who 'relapsed' and were newly registered or had some other change in register status were seen most often in each month, with a peak in the second and third months after the initial conference. Cases who remained on the register throughout the follow-up were seen next most

Fig 9.i
Social Work
Contact
& Register
Status

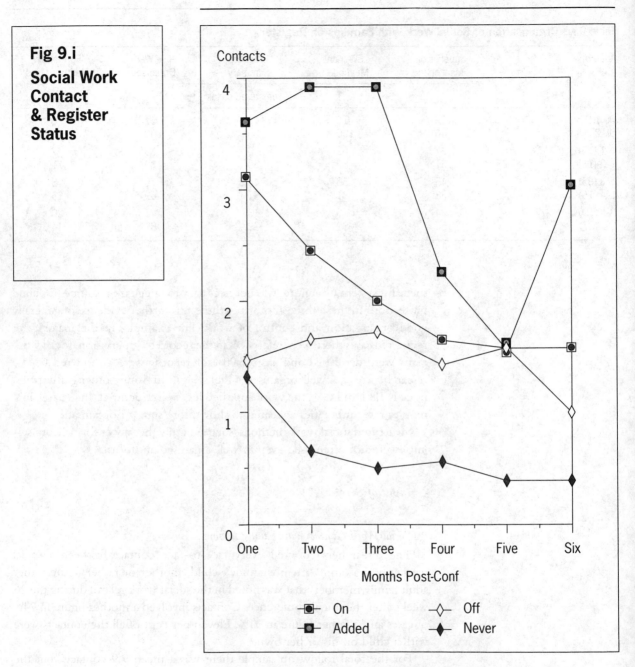

frequently: contacts peaked in the first month following the conference and then declined, levelling out at just under two a month in the fourth post-conference month. Cases who were removed from the register had less contact, and those who were never registered least of all. If a correction is made for cases who moved, the average number of contacts for the last three months increases slightly.

The total number of face-to-face contacts between social workers and one or more family members, and differences between the authority 'pairs' are illustrated in table 9v, showing contacts between social workers and cases who were and were not placed on the register at the initial conference. Initial register status clearly determined the amount of subsequent contact in all the authorities, but there were significant differences between them: in general, the 'low-rate' authorities had more contacts with cases remaining on the register. IL 2 had a particularly high rate of contact – an average 23.3 interviews over the six month follow-up, compared with an average of nine interviews in the strike-hit IL 1.

We can crudely measure the *continuity* of contact between social workers and families of children on the register by counting the number of four week periods in the follow-up without any contacts. For this exercise we looked only at cases still open at 26 weeks where all the children were still in the same authority. Table 9vi shows the mean number of periods, out of a possible seven, when there were no contacts between social worker and family members. The lower the number, the greater the continuity. There were significant differences in practice between the authorities, with IL 1 (because of the strike) showing most gaps in contact and IL 2 a striking degree of continuity of contact with cases on the register.

We attempted to rate the main *purpose* of each contact, in so far as this was made clear in the record. In each of the 7 follow-up periods, a rating was made of the *'importance'* of each purpose. An *'important'* purpose meant one that occurred in the majority of contacts in that particular period. Thus if a purpose was rated as 'important' in each of the seven periods, it would receive

Table 9.v. **Social Workers' Contacts with Child & Family in 6 Months Post-Conference**

Authority	On CPR	Added	Removed	Never On
	Mean contacts in 6 months			
OL 1 (32)	9.3	17.5	–	1.7
OL 2 (24)	13.2	–	13.0	3.2
IL 1 (26)	9.0	–	0	3.4
IL 2 (25)	23.3	–	18.5	11.4
IL 3 (56)	16.3	29.0	–	6.8
IL 4 (31)	17.7	30.0	9.3	4.6
C 1 (142)	10.9	14.7	3.9	4.2
C 2 (48)	15.6	11.0	10.9	2.3
ALL (384)	13.2	19.7	9.4	4.3
Missing data on 15 cases				

Difference in contact between different CPR statuses: F 22.68 df 3 sig. <.0001

Table 9.vi. **Continuity of Social Work Contact in Different Authorities**

Authority	Initial Conference Decision	
	Register	Not Register
	Months without contact	
OL 1 (19)	2.3	3.4
OL 2 (16)	2.1	3.6
IL 1 (19)	4.2	4.7
IL 2 (16)	0.8	3.7
IL 3 (41)	2.1	3.4
IL 4 (20)	2.0	4.0
C 1 (103)	2.6	3.15
C 2 (26)	2.0	2.6

Differences between authorities: F3.96 sig. 0004

a total score of 7. The identified purposes in respect of children initially placed on the register were as follows, in rank order of their *importance*.

● Arranging, discussing or negotiating the provision of services.

● Monitoring, checking on the child's safety or progress.

● Making specific protective arrangements or agreements in respect of the child, including discussing child protection conference decisions.

● 'Family casework' – listening, counselling etc

● Carrying out or discussing specific legal intervention, including arrangements for supervised access.

● Investigating or assessing the child or family members.

There were significant differences between authorities in respect to the importance given to *specific protection, casework, arranging services* and *investigation*. In IL 2, IL 3 and C 2, purposes concerned with specific protection and legal intervention were more important, although C 2 also showed the greatest concentration on *family casework*, and IL 2 combined its focus on protection with a high rating for *liaison and arranging services*.

The Provision of Family Support Services

A 'family support service' was defined as any service (other than 'ordinary' contacts with social work or health professionals) provided for a member of the family, including local authority services (such as financial help, a family aide, day care, family centre etc), services from other agencies (such as child guidance, psychiatric care, speech therapy, special education etc), voluntary services (such as Home-Start, NSPCC etc) or privately purchased services.

Table 9.vii. **Family Support Services Offered and Taken-Up During Follow-up**

Type of Service	Number Offered	% Partial/Full Takeup
Financial	198	99
Child Psychiatry OP	57	75.5
Child Accommodated	48	100
Day Nursery	49	85
Medical OP	28	79
Family Centre	24	87.5
Other Counselling	22	92
Help in House	21	85
Other Day Care	21	99
Adult Psychiatry OP	21	95
Other Residential	17	62.5
Other Educational	13	91
Alcohol/Drug Treatment	13	92
Given/Loaned Goods	12	73
Holiday	11	56
Other Voluntary Organisation	9	43
Volunteer Befriender	9	80
Adult Psychiatry IP	7	100
Remedial Teaching	3	67
Club	2	100
Medical IP	1	100
Boarding School	2	50
Marriage Guidance	1	100
Child Psychiatry IP	1	NK
Other	24	75
ALL	616	89

The results may well under-estimate the services provided (especially by other agencies) but they are unlikely to over-estimate them. The types of service offered and the recorded take-up by clients are shown in table 9vii.

Only 66 offers of service were not taken up at all. In about half, the reason was the client's refusal and in another third the service was not available.

The service-provider was the social services department in 59% of cases, the health authority in 18%, the voluntary sector in 13% and the education authority in 5%. Other sources provided the remaining 5%. The help most frequently provided by the social services department was financial and material help and day care for children. The financial help usually consisted of relatively small sums of money given to buy food, clothes or goods needed for children such as cots and nappies. The social services department thus was dependent on the resources of other agencies in a high proportion of cases, and this was especially so if therapeutic, education or other specialist forms of help were to be mobilised. While the services under the direct control of the department could nearly always be provided, this was not always the case with those controlled by other agencies. Remedial educational resources in particular were hard to obtain.

The services provided were usually aimed specifically towards the child (30%), or the parent figure and the child (25%). Twenty-one per cent were aimed at the whole family and only 18% were for the parent figures only.

The main purpose of the service was categorised as *practical* in 37%, *respite* in 16%, *counselling or therapy* in 14%, *assessment* in 11%, *parenting support* in 7%. Other purposes accounted for the remaining 15%.

There were significant differences in the provision of supportive services in different authorities, with two inner London authorities in particular (IL 2 and IL 4) providing higher than expected amounts. IL 2, for example, had 6.5% of the follow-up cases but provided 12.6% of the total number of services, nearly twice as many as would be expected.

Who Received Services?

We have seen that 'register status' was the main determinant of the amount of contact between social worker and family members. Did families where children were placed on the register also receive more supportive services than the other families considered at the initial CP conference? Register status largely determined a family's chances of receiving supportive services, with children on the register being more than three times as likely to be offered one. There were differences between authorities in the amount of service provision but all eight showed the same pattern of discrimination in favour of registered children. However, the average number of services offered obscures the very real differences between types of service: the offer of a few pounds to buy nappies might be expected to have very different results from the offer of specialised, continuing educational help. More detailed analysis showed that children placed on the register and their families obtained significantly more of only six types of service. These were:

- day nurseries (16% v. 4%)
- accommodation (16% v. 6%)
- adult psychiatry outpatient care (8% v. 2%)
- financial help (30% v. 15%)
- family aide (7% v. 3%)
- educational help other than boarding school or remedial teaching (6% v. 1%)

Children placed on the register were actually slightly less likely to be referred to child psychiatrists (13% v. 16%) and were about as likely to be referred for other counselling help (7% v. 6%) or to family centres (8% v. 4%). These results are in line with those of other studies of routine child protection services in showing that relatively little use is made of specialised services to promote the normal development of children who have experienced mal-treatment (Gough et al., 1987).

Levels of Legal Intervention

Legal actions taken by the authorities to protect children were classified in the following way:

- No legal action taken or considered in the initial conference plan – 283 cases (74% of cases with data available).
- Legal action considered in the initial conference plan but never taken – 23 cases (6%).
- Legal action taken before initial conference but legal orders no longer in force at 26 week follow-up – 18 cases (5%).
- Legal action planned at initial conference, or taken before it, and legal orders still in force 26 weeks later – 38 cases (10%)
- Legal orders in force after 26 weeks arising from post-conference incidents – 20 cases (5%).

Thus some legal action was taken at some stage in 20% of conferenced cases and in 15% legal orders were in force 26 weeks after the initial conference.

Register status was strongly related to legal intervention: only 9% of cases not placed on the register received any legal intervention, compared with 34% of those on it.

There were marked differences in levels of legal intervention in different authorities. In general, the outer London boroughs, the counties and IL 4 made less use of legal intervention than did the remaining three inner London boroughs.

Patterns of Service

We searched for different styles or patterns of service delivery. If there was neither legal intervention nor supportive services the style of service delivery was called *'low provision'*. If there was legal intervention with no family support provision the style was called *'enforcing'*. *'Supportive'* described a style of service delivery that used no legal intervention but did provide family support services. Finally, a combination of legal intervention and provision of family support was called *'controlling support'* (Table 9viii). A *Supportive* style was most commonly used in cases ever on the register, while *low provision* was most common for conferenced cases not placed on the register. *Enforcement* (legal action without any family support provision) was rare. *Controlling*

Table 9.viii. **Patterns of Service Delivery**

Pattern	Ever on CPR	Never on CPR	All
Low Provision	64 (26)	65 (47)	129 (34)
Enforcing	12 (5)	8 (6)	20 (5)
Supportive	117 (48)	59 (43)	176 (46)
Controlling Support	50 (21)	6 (4)	56 (15)
ALL	243 (100)	138 (100)	381 (100)
Missing data on 17 cases			

Service patterns v. CPR status: chi sq = 27.6 df 3 sig.<.0001

support was approximately 5 times as common in cases placed on the register, but was used in only 20% even of these.

However, there were marked differences between authorities. IL 3 was unusual in the frequency with which it used an *enforcing* style of service delivery – 20% of its families receiving this style compared to the average of 5%. IL 2 stood out for the infrequency with which it used *low provision* as a style – for only 15% of families compared to the average of 34%. The marked differences in style between the 'paired' authorities IL 1 and IL 2 (with IL 1 relying more on *low provision*) may have been due to the effects of the strike in IL 1. The differences between IL 3 and IL 4 (with IL 4 never using *enforcement* and more often using a *supportive* style) were more likely to reflect genuine differences in policy and practice.

In summary, we have seen that the eight authorities differed in their ability to comply with recommended child protection procedures – notably in allocating keyworkers for continuous periods, in holding child protection reviews and in involving parents. In three 'low-rate' authorities (one outer and one inner London borough and one county) recommended procedures were mostly followed, while they were largely inoperative in another borough where social workers were on strike. Authorities also differed in the amount and continuity of contact between social workers and families of children placed on the register. However in all of them the pattern was the same: register status had a determining influence on the service offered in the six months following the initial conference. Registration in all authorities ensured increased social work contact and provision of support services: the difference between them was one of degree. A 'supportive' style of child protection with little use of legal intervention was the most commonly found in all authorities, but again there were differences of degree with one inner London borough showing greater preference for an 'enforcing' style.

Although families where a child was placed on the register were generally in regular contact with a social worker and also received additional supportive services over the following six months, most did not receive help which was specifically geared to helping the child overcome the effects of maltreatment or to enabling the parents to provide more adequate care. The prevailing form of service was a general monitoring of the family combined with practical help of a limited kind.

Chapter 10

Children's Outcomes Six Months after Initial Protection Conferences

In this chapter we shall examine three indicators of 'outcome':

● removal of children's names from the register;

● the extent of repeated suspected maltreatment;

● the separation of children from their own parents.

We recognise that six months is a very short follow-up period. We must also bear in mind the limitations of these outcome indicators, since they cannot show actual change within families or their members' own views of change.

Removal of Children from the Register

Thirty cases (some 13% of those originally registered) had been removed from the register 26 weeks after the initial conference. There were marked differences between authorities: IL 2 removed most (35% of those initally registered), followed by C 2 (27%), IL 4 (17%) and C 1 (12%). In IL 3 and OL 1 no cases had been removed from the register and less than 10% in OL 2 and IL 1. Thus the use of the child protection register appeared more purposeful in IL 2 and C 2: there was higher turnover, presumably related to more focused assessments of whether the child still needed protection. These two authorities, as we have already seen, were also the ones adhering most closely to recommended child protection procedures. In these authorities keyworkers were allocated for a continuous period, the work was well organised, child protection reviews were held at which the need for continuing protection was critically reviewed. The result seemed to be that children remained on the register for shorter periods.

Repetition of Abuse or Neglect

We have shown that authorities differed widely in their compliance with recommended procedures, in levels of contact between social workers and families and in the provision of support services. Were these differences reflected in repetition rates? For example, were children in the 'best' authorities (IL 2 and C 2) less likely to suffer repeated maltreatment than those in the 'worst' authority, IL 1, where only a skeleton service was provided due to the social worker strike, but where children on the register were monitored by other agencies and discussed at managerial meetings?

Table 10.i **Repeated Suspected Abuse or Neglect in 26 Week Follow-Up**

Authority	Mean Repeats		% With a Repeat	
	On CPR	Not On CPR	On CPR	Not On CPR
OL 1 (32)	.40	.17	20	18
OL 2 (24)	.60	0	40	0
IL 1 (26)	.60	.36	40	27
IL 2 (25)	.35	.12	29	12.5
IL 3 (58)	.51	.36	27	25
IL 4 (30)	.25	0	25	6
C 1 (139)	.66	.54	35.5	31
C 2 (48)	.70	.63	41	18
ALL (382)	.51	.29	31	19

Numbers in brackets. Missing data on 17 cases
Mean repeats: registered v. not registered: $F=4.75$ sig .029
Mean repeats: authority differences: $F=1.16$ sig .32

Details were taken of all further reports of supected physical or sexual abuse or neglect during the 26 week follow-up period. The results are shown in Table 10i. On average, there was a repeated episode of suspected abuse or negect in 31% of cases originally placed on the register and 19% of those not originally registered. Corby (1987) reported that 28% of a small follow-up sample repeated abuse within two years. The mean number of repeated allegations in cases originally placed on the register was .51, versus .29 for those not originally registered – a statistically significant difference. This might suggest that inital conferences were registering the right children – those most at risk – or that because of the closer monitoring of children on the register, suspected ill-treatment was more likely to be reported.

There were no significant differences between authorities in the number of repeated episodes or the proportion of cases with a repeat. Thus, in spite of the different patterns of practice in the different authorities, their outcome in terms of crude numbers of further episodes of suspected abuse or neglect was similar. It may be, however, that cases were less closely monitored in IL 1 and that more repetitions occurred there than came to official attention.

Children who were originally referred for neglect were somewhat more likely to raise further concerns during the follow-up (36% compared to 26% of those referred for physical abuse and 25% for sexual abuse). Re-referrals did not relate closely to the original concerns. For example, for 10 of the 50 'physical abuse' children who were re-referred the new allegations concerned sexual abuse and for 17 they concerned neglect or other maltreatment than physical injury. The families who gave rise to continuing concerns thus tended to show a general failure of parental care rather than a specific pattern of abuse.

In 20% of the re-referred cases, the concerns were about risks rather than actual incidents. In 42% there had been an alleged incident but it was not particularly serious – for example there had been no physical contact in the case of alleged further sexual abuse, or only a bruise in the case of repeated physical injury. However, in the remaining 38% of cases the repeated allegations were rated as serious, involving extreme physical neglect, more serious injuries or physical sexual contacts. In two of these cases there was a fatal outcome – although one of these children died as a result of the original injury not in consequence of a further one.

Once again the problem arises of distinguishing between allegations that were and were not confirmed. We looked more closely at the reported incidents to distinguish those where the concerns had apparently been substantiated by investigation. Just over half the suspected repeated incidents were substantiated – very similar to the proportion of the initial incidents substantiated. Counting only substantiated incidents as 'repeats' did not affect the finding that there were no significant differences between authorities.

Removal of Children from Home

By the end of the follow-up period, of the children *not* originally placed on the register 71% had remained at home throughout, 15% had left for a period but returned and 14% had left and were still away. Of the cases originally *placed* on the register, 63% had remained continuously at home, 18% had left but returned and 19% had left and were still away. There were no significant differences between authorities in these proportions.

Outcome Status in Eight Authorities: Summary

We will now try to summarise the position of the conferenced children after 26 weeks. We classified the children's outcome status into one of six possible categories.

- *Safe at Home*: The child was with at least one parent (not necessarily the same one as at the initial incident) and was 'safe', in the sense that no further maltreatment had been substantiated.

- *At Home: Further Harm*: The child was with at least one parent but was less 'safe', in that further harm had been substantiated.

- *Safe: Accommodated*: The child was accommodated or living with relatives but no further harm had been substantiated.

- *Removed After Further Harm*: The child had been separated from both parents during the follow-up as the result of further harm or a legal order – that is, the original plan of maintaining the child at home had broken down.

- *Removed Initially*: The child had been separated from both parents before or at the time of the initial conference and was still away 26 weeks later.

- *Death*: The child had died.

Table 10iiA illustrates the outcome status of children who were originally placed on the register. Altogether, 57% were safely at home with at least one parent 26 weeks after the initial conference. The numbers were too small for the differences between authorities to have statistical significance.

Table 10.iiA. **Outcome in Different Authorities: Remaining Safely at Home**

Authority	Home Safe	Home Harm	Removed/ Harm	Contin. Away	Left Home No Harm	Died
	% cases origionally placed on register					
OL 1(15)	60	20	13	0	7	0
OL 2 (10)	60	10	20	10	0	0
IL 1 (15)	47	20	20	13	0	0
IL 2 (17)	59	17	12	6	6	0
IL 3 (33)	61	21	3	15	0	0
IL 4 (16)	69	13	6	6	6	0
C 1 (100)	61	28	4	6	0	1
C 2 (26)	31	31	11	23	4	0
ALL (232)	57	24	8	9	2	<1

Missing data on 9 cases. Numbers in brackets
Difference between authorities: chi sq=36.7 df 35 sig.=.38

The outcome status of children who were not placed on the register is shown in table 10iiB. Conferenced children who were not placed on the register by the initial conference were significantly more likely to remain 'safely' with a parent. Seventy-three per cent of those *not* registered were so classified compared with 57% of those registered (using chi square statistic, $P< .003$). IL 1, however, was an exception in that slightly fewer of those not registered than of those registered ended up safely with a parent after six months: rather more broke down or were continuously away. With this exception, children not registered by the initial conference appeared to have significantly better outcomes, again suggesting that in general conferences were tending to register those most at risk.

Table 10.iiB. **Outcome in Different Authorities: Remaining Safely at Home**

Authority	Home Safe	Home Harm	Removed/ Harm	Contin. Away	Left Home No Harm	Died
	% cases not placed on register					
OL 1(17)	82	18	0	0	0	0
OL 2 (14)	93	0	0	0	7	0
IL 1 (11)	46	18	9	27	0	0
IL 2 (8)	62.5	12.5	0	12.5	12.5	0
IL 3 (25)	68	16	4	8	0	4
IL 4 (16)	93	0	7	0	0	0
C 1 (39)	67	26	2	0	5	0
C 2 (26)	73	18	0	4.5	4.5	0
ALL (150)	73	16	3	6	2	<1

Missing data on 8 cases. Numbers in brackets
Difference between authorities: chi sq=40.7 df 35 sig.=.23

The Meaning of a 'Good Outcome' in Child Protection Work

Most people would probably agree that a maltreated child living safely at home six months after a child protection conference had a better outcome than a child who was removed after repetition of maltreatment, or who never returned home. However, we are not comparing like with like: the children who broke down or were never returned home differed in a number of ways from the others. The main differences were in:

● Age-group. Two groups were particularly likely to break down or remain separated: under-fives and teenagers.

● Reason for referral. Children originally notified for neglect or concerns about parents' ability to care were more likely to break down or remain separated.

● Poverty. Although, as we have seen, most of the families were disadvantaged, those who broke down had significantly more poverty indicators.

● Parental characteristics. Families where one or both parents abused alcohol or drugs or where there was domestic violence were more likely to break down or remain separated (compare Famularo et al, 1992).

● Previous maltreatment. When there had been previous investigations the risk of breakdown was significantly higher.

Seventy-eight percent of children with none or only one of the indicators of poor prognosis remained safely at home, compared with 71% of children with two prognostic indicators and 45% of those with three or more. Twelve per cent of 'good prognosis' children remained at home with suspected further harm but 32% of 'poor prognosis' children did so. Only 9% of 'good prognosis' children were separated from both parents after six months, compared to 23% of 'poor prognosis' children.

There were marked differences in these prognostic factors between the eight authorities (shown in table 10iii), with conferenced children in some having a worse prognosis, on average, than in others. IL 1, IL 2 and C 2 conferenced the most 'poor prognosis' children, and C 1 and OL 2 the fewest.

There were significant differences between authorities in the outcome statuses of children with poor prognoses – not in those with good or moderate prognoses. Considering the 'paired' authorities, in OL 1, 73% of children with poor prognoses remained safely at home, compared to 25% in OL 2. The comparable figures for IL 1 and IL 2 were 29% versus 40%. For IL 3 and IL 4 they were 54% versus 70%; and for C 1 and C 2 they were 44% versus 33%. OL 1 and IL 4 stood out as maintaining more children with poor prognoses 'safely' in their own homes. Thus those authorities who adhered most closely to recommended child protection procedures (IL 2 and C 2) did not have 'better' outcomes, even after controlling for prognostic factors.

Intervention to protect children cannot be expected to work miracles and transform family situations characterised by violent parents abusing drugs and alcohol, who have a long-standing pattern of incapacity for parenting and very few material resources, into safe and nurturing environments. In these circumstances the meaning of 'a good outcome' for child and parent must be re-thought. What would be a 'least bad' outcome at six months? First, we

Table 10.iii. **Indicators of Poor Prognosis Among Conferenced Children in Different Authorities**

Authority	Home at 6 Months	Remained Separated	All
	Mean prognostic indicators		
OL 1 (31)	2.07	1.0	2.03
OL 2 (24)	1.09	3.67	1.41
IL 1 (25)	2.56	4.33	3.2
IL 2 (25)	2.66	4.25	2.92
IL 3 (57)	2.08	3.37	2.23
IL 4 (28)	1.84	3.67	2.04
C 1 (133)	1.85	2.0	1.84
C 2 (47)	2.43	3.1	2.57
ALL (370)	2.01	3.27	2.16

Some data missing on 29 cases

Differences between authorities: F 3.81 DF 7 sig. .0005

suggest, the child should be **safe in a family setting**, either her or his own or, if that would not be safe, in an alternative family. Second, there should be **clear plans for the child's future** so s/he does not become 'lost in care'. Third, **links with his or her immediate and extended family** should be preserved where this is at all possible. Fourth, **appropriate help** should be mobilised to compensate for any developmental delays or problems the child may experience as a result of maltreatment.

'Least Bad' Outcomes

We may now review the children who were not re-united with their parents from this point of view. Did they achieve as good outcomes as might be expected, considering their poor prognosis? We shall look separately at the under-fives and the teenagers.

All 18 of the under-fives who were not with a parent after six months were in family settings – about half with a member of the extended family. Clear plans for the future existed for all except three, and contact with one or more family members was being maintained for all except three – all these were in IL 1, where normal practice was interrupted by the strike. Randomly-chosen examples illustrate the generally satisfactory outcomes of the separated under-fives:

Case 844 was an about-to-be-born baby, referred by a Homeless Persons' Unit. Mother had a serious psychiatric illnes and there were concerns about her ability to care for a child. There had been previous investigations for physical abuse and the four other children were now with the former husband. The father of the new baby was another patient met in the psychiatric hospital. The Social Services obtained a legal order on the child's birth and he was taken to a foster home. The key worker assisted the couple to maintain regular contact, although this was disrupted by their relapse and re-admission to hospital. Rehabilitation was considered impossible and placement in the extended family was being explored with a view to adoption.

Case 467 was a four year old boy found by police wandering in the main road naked from the waist down. The police found father drunk and mother 'spaced out' at home. The flat was filthy and there was very little food. There had been at least two previous investigations for abuse and neglect. Both parents abused drugs and alcohol and mother was diabetic and epileptic, needing frequent hospital admissions. The child was developmentally delayed, with hardly any speech. The conference plan was for the child to remain in accommodation with a legal order being sought if parents tried to remove him. The child made gains in speech and social skills in foster care after a proper developmental assessment was obtained and the keyworker provided support for the parents and helped them maintain an erratic contact. Then mother died. The keyworker helped father and the other children through their mourning and her continued efforts to engage the family in work to improve their situation were beginning to bear fruit by the end of the follow-up. The child was still accommodated in foster care but rehabilitation was the ultimate aim.

Case 774 was a newborn baby. Mother had been sexually abused and taken into care as a child. She had myotonic dystrophy and learning difficulties. She was homeless and alone, had money problems and was abusing drugs. The conference plan was for mother to be accommodated with the baby in hospital where her ability to care could be assessed.

Mother did not comply with the arrangements and repeatedly left the baby on the ward. The Social Services obtained an Interim Care Order and moved the child to a foster home encouraging mother to have supervised contact four times a week. Mother did attend but showed little understanding of the baby's needs, so the review CPC decided to proceed with a full Care Order and adoption plans. The situation was changed by the appearance of a new partner and the keyworker agreed to conduct a new assessment. The keyworker maintained careful liaison with the many parties involved and at the end of the follow-up the child was in the same foster home under a full Care Order with assessment for rehabilitation in progress and a contingency plan for adoption if rehabilitation could not be achieved.

By contrast, the outcomes of the teenagers separated from parents was less good. Of the 16, five were in residential units and one was in a psychiatric hospital. In only a third could a clear plan for the future be identified and many had lost contact with their families. Less careful planning seemed to be undertaken with this age group, and yet they were in a very vulnerable position, in danger of drifting into homelessness with no means of earning a reasonable living. It was difficult for social workers and other professionals to make an impact on the situation since the problems were usually entrenched, there were often warring family members with different interests (for example, new cohabitees or step-parents) and the child him or herself was no longer a helpless baby who could be moved at will, but an often truculent and unpredictable young person.

Case 1564 was a 14 year old girl who revealed that her brother had buggered her some years previously. He admitted this. The girl had previously been on the register for emotional abuse. The conference plan was for a full family assessment and cautioning of the brother. However, the case was closed after only one home visit. The following month the child was investigated in hospital for a bowel complaint and was behaving in a strange manner. She later requested accommodation and was admitted to a children's home but two weeks later the case conference core group decided she should go home. She refused and when unable to sway the professionals she tried to hang herself. Soon after this she disclosed sexual abuse by her father. At follow-up she was still in the children's home.

Case 1092 was a 15 year old girl who requested accommodation claiming she was hit by father in drunken rages. She was taken to a children's home. The conference plan is unknown since no minutes were taken. There was minimal input from the keyworker and at follow-up she was still accommodated in the children's home with no record of any plans for the future.

Case 1684 was a 14 year old girl referred by a family friend to whom the child had run away, saying mother's cohabitee had touched her breasts. Mother requested the child be taken into care as she did not believe her allegations. There were many family problems. The conference plan was for the child to stay in foster care while further investigation was carried out and contact re-established with mother. The residential worker was supposed to be offering counselling but disappeared on sick leave. The foster placement broke down and the girl moved to a children's home. Her mother remained hostile and no contact was established. At follow-up the child remained in the children's home but there was a possible plan to establish contact with the family she had run away to in the first place. It seemed remiss not to have done this at the beginning, six months previously.

Case 769 was a 14 year old boy taken to a foster home under a place of safety order after becoming involved in a knife fight with mother and her estranged husband. The parents had separated and the child had recently been expelled from boarding school and returned by father to mother. The conference plan was to maintain the boy in voluntary care and work towards rehabilitation with mother over the next couple of weeks, as well as mobilising educational and psychiatric help. The social worker went on extended leave immediately and there was no contact for several months. The recommended resources were never secured and the boy remained accommodated in the foster home at follow-up with no clear plans for the future.

Elements of Good Social Work Practice

There seemed to be common elements to cases showing a reasonably good outcome after six months, taking into account a generally poor prognosis. First, the initial child protection conference needed to make a *clear plan that was capable of being fulfilled, taking into account the history and current problems.* A flexible approach allowing for different contingencies was necessary, not a rigid plan to be imposed whatever the change in circumstances or people's reactions.

Secondly, *a social worker needed to be allocated from the start and to involve the parents and child (when able to speak) from the beginning in the carrying out of the plan.* This was made more difficult if no social worker had been allocated to carry out the investigation and the family had had to cope with a succession of duty workers. Then, family members did not often attend initial conferences and so had no chance to contribute to the plan. A keyworker was not always allocated at once and there could be a gap of several weeks between the initial conference and the keyworker's first visit to the family. Any momentum that could have been achieved from the conference proceedings was lost.

Thirdly, *the social worker needed to build personal relationships of trust and respect with all the key parties.* The emphasis on 'making relationships' that used to be so central to social work practice has probably gone and some social workers may give less priority to the skills and attitudes needed to do this. We feel convinced that child protection work hinges to a considerable extent on the social worker's skill in engaging the co-operation of others and this requires an investment in personal relationships. Some keyworkers were particularly skilled in maintaining relationships with several members of the immediate and extended family, even when these people hated and distrusted each other. When this could be done it opened up many more possibilities of help for the child.

Fourthly, the social worker needed to *mobilise appropriate practical and specialist help* at an early stage in order to relieve the severe stress that affected so many of the families and to inject some hope and energy into the situation.

Fifthly, the members of the conference, the social worker and the agency sometimes needed *courage to confront dangerous adults and take decisive protective action* rather than collude with continuing harm being inflicted on children.

These qualities and skills seemed more important than technical social work methods, which were rarely used, and also more important than comprehensive assessments in the form recommended by the Department of Health (1988), which were more often undertaken. All too often these seemed to become an end in themselves, never feeding back into the child protection plan nor actually influencing what was done. Two brief examples will illustrate these notions of the components of good practice.

Case 1227 was a 13 year old girl who came to attention because of neighbours' allegations that she was living alone with her unemployed father as man and wife. The school was also concerned at her withdrawn behaviour and frequent absences. At first the child denied all the allegations. Then she agreed to a medical examination which confirmed that regular sexual intercourse had taken place. Confronted with this, she agreed that she and father were lovers and said that 'no-one knew how special their love was'. She was distraught by being moved to a foster home and not allowed to see father, who was held in custody and charged with incest. The conference plan was to seek a Care Order and prevent contact with father, while trying to trace the child's mother. The social worker established a close and supportive relationship with the child, allowing her to decide the pace of disclosure and how much to tell. The social worker contacted members of the extended family to piece together her history for the child, and arranged for contact with her mother, stepfather and stepsiblings. She visited the father in prison to confront him over his expressed determination to get hold of his daughter again as soon as he was released, which she tried to counter by having the child made a ward of court. The father then wrote her threatening letters at the time of her own marriage, which she dealt with firmly by complaining to the prison governor. The child appeared to be overcoming the past and was reported by the school to be 'blossoming'. Six months after the conference she was accommodated in the foster home, with wardship pending, and the possibility of rehabilitation with her mother was being explored.

Case 258 concerned a nine year old girl who told her aunt she wouldn't go back home after witnessing mother stab her cohabitee in a row over money for drinking. There had been similar violent incidents when she had run to friends' houses. The child was adamant that she wanted to live with the aunt because mother didn't care for her and she was frightened by drinking and fighting and men sleeping in the flat. The housing office confirmed that the flat was a suspected brothel and that the child had been seen outside at 2.0 am. Mother had been convicted of prostitution offences and cohabitee also had a criminal record. Both abused alcohol and there were many financial problems. The conference plan was to apply for a Care Order and assess the placement with the aunt in the hope that it could be maintained. The keyworker became involved with various members of the extended family, keeping the balance and trying to maintain contact between mother and daughter, while laying down firm conditions that would have to be met before she could return home. Mother did not keep agreements over seeking help for drinking and could not stick to contact arrangements. In six months the child was settled with her aunt under a Care Order and the aunt intended to apply for a residence order with parental responsibility.

In summary, judging the outcome of child protection intervention is a complex and difficult matter. An 'administrative' indicator like time to de-registration showed clear differences between different authorities, with the better-organised ones discharging more children from the register within six months. However, when indicators of 'failure', such as repeated suspected maltreatment or longer-term separation from parents, were examined no significant differences between authorities could be demonstrated. On average 57% of children placed on the register remained safely at home after six months as against 73% of children not originally registered. This might suggest that authorities were tending to register the 'right' children – those who most needed protection.

Babies and teenagers were more likely to remain separated, as were children from families marked by extreme poverty, where parents abused alcohol or drugs, there was domestic violence and previous investigations for neglect or abuse had been undertaken. Authorities differed in the proportions of conferenced children with these characteristics: some were faced with more difficult problems than others and achieved success in the face of greater odds.

'Success', in the case of children with poor prognoses, was more meaningfully evaluated by indicators of the child's safety; future security and maintenance of family contacts than by a single crude indicator such as repeated investigation for maltreatment. When outcomes were examined in this way, most authorities (with the exception of one where work was affected by a prolonged strike) were found to be achieving satisfactory results with under-fives, but less good results with teenagers.

Chapter 11

Conclusions

In this final chapter we shall summarise the principal results of the study before considering their implications for policies on child protection.

Variation in the Operation of Central Child Protection Registers

The study was commissioned first, to document the extent of variation in the way central registers were operated and used within the child protection system. This was studied by means of a postal survey of English registers (reported in chapter 2). The survey confirmed the existence of wide variations in the criteria for entry to the registers and the data held on them. Interpreting the categories and deciding on appropriate thresholds for their application caused some difficulties for authorities, particularly in relation to 'Grave Concern' – a category subsequently abolished by the Department of Health. Authorities differed in their understanding of the fundamental purpose of the register: some still saw it as a record of documented abuse in the past, rather than as a record of inter-agency plans that were *currently* necessary to protect a child. Thus some authorities included dead children's names on the register and maintained an 'intermediate category' of children who had no inter-agency protection plans.

Operational factors reflecting register definitions and criteria, inefficiency due to resource problems, and more general organisational patterns were found to discriminate between registers with high and low rates of children on them. In combination, these factors acted to raise artificially the rates of children on the register.

Most respondents believed that central registers were an essential part of the child protection system. Registers received on average 281 enquiries in six months (with wide variations).

They were used to provide management information, maintain inter-agency co-ordination and support practice. Central registers were generally seen to be useful parts of local systems to improve the detection and prevention of child maltreatment. However, without greater standardisation of procedures to improve reliability, national statistics of children on registers are likely to be misleading in comparing different parts of the country or comparing trends over time.

Eight Authorities: Characteristics of Referred Children

The second objective of the research was to describe variation in the processes that led to a child's name being placed on the register. More detailed study in four 'pairs' of authorities – two outer London boroughs, four inner London boroughs and two counties – was undertaken for this purpose and the methods are described in chapter 3. Over a 16 week period, children referred for investigations were identified, and their progress through the child protection system was tracked through social work records and minutes of conferences.

The characteristics of the referred children and their families are described in chapters 3 and 4. Most of the 1,888 referrals (44%) were for suspected physical abuse, followed by suspected sexual abuse (28%), and neglect (21%) or fears for the child's safety (4%). Only 3% of referrals involved allegations of emotional abuse without other forms of maltreatment.

Less than a third of children lived with both natural parents and there were high levels of social deprivation, though children investigated for sexual or emotional abuse were in generally better material circumstances. About two-thirds of the families were already known to the social services department, and nearly half had experienced previous investigations for abuse or neglect. A substantial minority of parents had histories of criminal behaviour, substance abuse or mental illness. Domestic violence was recorded in over a quarter.

Very few allegations of physical abuse involved serious physical injury, but nevertheless, this small minority included five deaths – only two of which led to court proceedings.

In allegations of sexual abuse (involving some form of physical contact in over half the cases), the children were older and the ratio of girls to boys was 1.85:1. Boys were more often the subject of allegations of physical abuse and neglect.

The alleged perpetrators of physical and sexual abuse also differed. Males were accused in 96% of sexual abuse referrals, but only 53% of physical abuse ones. Nearly 90% of alleged perpetrators of physical abuse were natural or substitute parents, while approaching half the alleged perpetrators of sexual abuse were not related to the child (though they were rarely strangers). Nearly a quarter of them were under 18 – a prevalence of young abusers similar to that found in a more systematic prevalence study in N. Ireland (Royal Belfast Hospital, 1990), and in Finkelhor's survey of American college students, where one in four of those who had been sexually abused in childhood described the perpetrator as an adolescent (Finkelhor, 1979). Organised abuse was extremely rare.

Unsubstantiated Allegations

The difficulties of deciding whether a reported concern about maltreatment was substantiated are discussed in chapter 5. Different levels of certainty were distinguished: the allegations were regarded as untrue; alternative explanations of the events were accepted; there were suspicions but the evidence was regarded as insufficient; and there was some or definite evidence of deliberate maltreatment. Just over half the allegations fell into this last category. The chances of substantiation were most influenced by whether the child confirmed the allegation (48% told about sexual abuse and 42% about physical abuse), but they were also affected by the source of the referral and its circumstances.

Filtering Cases out of the Child Protection System

The operation of the child protection system was conceived as a dynamic process. From the mass of possible 'cases' entering the system at referral, some had to be selected to be the subjects of inter-agency protection plans. Selection was carried out through successive organisational filters, described in chapter 6.

The first filter was operated by social work duty staff, often, but not always, in consultation with a senior worker and after making telephone enquiries of other agencies. About a quarter of the referrals were filtered out at this stage, without any direct contact with the child or family. Cases were more likely to disappear at this early stage if the allegations concerned neglect, rather than physical or sexual abuse, the abuse was physically less serious, the perpetrator was not in the household, the source of the referral was anonymous or a lay person and there had been no previous contact with social services.

The second filter was the investigation itself, with a senior social worker or manager usually being the crucial decision-maker. About two-thirds of the cases actually investigated were filtered out and never reached the initial child protection conference. The nature of the abuse incident and the source of referral were again influential, as were any previous history of suspected maltreatment and any recorded parental problems – such as criminality or substance abuse. Not many unsubstantiated cases with few indicators of 'risk' escaped the filters and reached the initial conference. However, a significant minority of substantiated cases with many 'risk' indicators, who perhaps needed to be considered by a conference, never reached one.

The third filter was operated by the membership of the initial protection conference and is described in chapter 7. On average, 7.4 professionals (excluding the chair) attended the conference, with (apart from social services staff) police officers and nurses being most often represented and doctors least often. Parents attended less than a fifth. In 51% of the conferenced cases the child was registered; 10% were deferred; 10% were already on the register; and the remaining 29% were not registered. Compared with those not registered, cases placed on the register had more previous investigations for abuse, more indicators of poverty and more parental deviance and domestic violence. Although cases of neglect were discriminated against by the first two filters, the few who reached the conference had an equal chance of being placed on the register. Certainty that abuse or neglect had occurred, its seriousness, and characteristics of the parents that might indicate future risk to the child made it more likely in all eight authorities that a case would be placed on the child protection register. Very few unsubstantiated, low-risk cases reached the register in any authority, but some cases with apparently great needs for protection were not registered – though they were not necessarily left unprotected.

The overall picture was of a pool of children and families about whom there was chronic concern on the part of community agencies. At various times, in response to a particularly serious incident or particular pressure from a powerful local agency, a family from this pool took its turn on the child protection register.

We conclude that on average some six out of every seven children who entered the system at referral were filtered out of it without needing to be placed on a child protection register. In a high proportion (44% of those actually investigated) the investigation led to no actions at all. There was no intervention to protect the child – for example by separating him or her from the alleged perpetrator – nor were any other family support services provided.

In only 4% of all the cases referred were children removed from home under a legal order during the investigation. The figure was slightly higher for neglect and physical abuse than for sexual abuse (3%). The practices revealed in Orkney (Clyde, 1992) are certainly not commonly used by social services departments.

Differences in Practice between the Eight Authorities

In each pair, one authority had higher official rates of children on the register. These differences could not be explained by differences in numbers of children referred into the child protection system. In the sample as a whole, inner London authorities had higher referral rates compared with outer London and the counties.

Within the paired authorities, the 'high-rate' one consistently identified more cases of sexual abuse and fewer cases of neglect. This difference in type of maltreatment was linked to differences in the age and gender of referred children and the source of referral.

There were other differences in the characteristics of children entering the child protection system in different areas, including the seriousness of the abuse triggering referral, racial background, family structure, poverty and parental problems. These differences did not discriminate between 'paired' authorities but between different types of authority, reflecting differences in local populations. However, cases identified in 'high-rate' authorities had more previous contact with social services, previous legal intervention and child protection investigations.

The eight authorities filtered different proportions of referrals out of the system at different stages. They differed in:

- the proportion of cases filtered out without investigative interview;
- the proportion investigated who were filtered out before the case conference;
- the conduct of the investigation;
- the proportion of conferenced cases placed on the register;
- the degree to which registration was targeted to cases with most risk indicators;
- the use of deferred decisions;

However, the differences between the 'paired' authorities were usually not statistically significant, especially when characteristics of referrals were taken into account. It is unlikely that differences in official rates of children on the register can be simply explained by differences in the way that referrals are processed in the different areas.

There were also differences in the way authorities applied recommended procedures, including:

- conference attendance;
- time taken to call a conference;
- the appointment of a keyworker;
- whether and when a child protection review was held;
- the involvement of parents;
- the services provided post-conference.

Differences in practice were not due to policy differences set out in Manuals of Procedure (except possibly for the involvement of parents). Formally prescribed procedures did not account for the observed differences in practice.

Effects of Registration

The ability of authorities to apply recommended child protection pro-cedures, the amount of contact between social worker and family members, the use of legal orders and the delivery of supportive services were examined in the six months after the initial conference (chapter 9). Within the paired authorities, the 'low-rate' ones generally demonstrated a more organised pattern of work and greater compliance with governmental guidance on the role of keyworkers and of the review conference.

In all the authorities, children on the register and their families, compared with those not registered, received significantly more contact with social workers, more legal intervention and more supportive services. However, relatively little use was made of specialised services to help promote the normal development of children affected by abuse. The prevailing form of service was a general monitoring of the family combined with practical help of a limited kind. The most common style was a supportive one, making no use of enforcement or legal control.

Outcomes

Outcomes of conferenced children after six months were described in chapter 10 using three main indicators:

- removal of a child's name from the register
- repeated suspected maltreatment
- removal of a child from home.

There were marked differences in the proportion of children de-registered after six months, ranging from 35% to none de-registered. The 'low-rate' authorities generally de-registered more children. It is likely that differences in the length of time children's names are kept on the register play a part in explaining the differences in official rates of children on registers, and this in turn is related to differences in the timing and use of child protection reviews.

On average, 31% of cases originally placed on the register and 19% of those not so placed experienced further suspected harm in the six months following the initial conference.

57% of those originally placed on the register were safely at home, with no reports of further harm, compared with 73% of those not registered. Children were less likely to be safely at home if they had been living in extreme poverty, there had been previous investigations for maltreatment, either parent abused alcohol or drugs and there was domestic violence. Under-fives and teenagers were most likely to remain separated after six months.

There were no statistically significant difference between authorities in the proportions remaining safely at home, in spite of the wide differences in their practices and services, but some of the authorities were dealing with children who had worse prognoses.

'Success', in the case of children with a poor prognosis, was more meaningfully evaluated by indicators of the child's safety, future security and maintenance of family contacts than by a single crude indicator, such as repeated investigation for maltreatment. When outcomes were examined in this way, most authorities were achieving good results with under-fives, but less so with teenagers.

The results of the study suggest that differences between the rate of children on the register in different areas cannot be easily attributed to a single cause. Lower-rate authorities did tend to operate child protection procedures in more selective ways and to have higher thresholds for registration, but there was also evidence of different thresholds between different types of authority – a relatively prosperous outer London borough setting a lower threshold than a very deprived inner London one. The evidence from the sample authorities suggested that the main influence on registration rates was the nature of the local population, the level of social deprivation and disorganis-ation and the local authority's response. But features of the child protection system, such as the relations between local agencies which affected the rate at which particular kinds of maltreatment were notified to the child protection system and policies on the way the central register was kept, were also important. At the practice level, low-rate authorities tended to be better organised and to de-register children more quickly, thus achieving more rapid turnover.

The authorities in the study appeared to be demonstrating more consist-ency in their decision-making than might have been expected. Although there were no written policies for the factors that should be taken into account when making decisions about registration, in all the authorities the same sort of children were being placed on the register. Registered children in all eight authorities tended to show many characteristics which could be described as 'common-sense' risk indicators. They had suffered from more serious, substantiated maltreatment over a longer period; the perpetrator had continuing access to them through being in the same household; there was domestic violence and the parent figures had characteristics such as crimi-nality, mental illness and drug or alcohol abuse. By contrast, lone parents in poverty who were referred because of concerns about their ability to care adequately for their children were likely to be filtered out of the child protection system in all authorities, usually without the offer of other services.

Discussion

The local study was planned as a monitoring exercise in selected 'pairs' of authorities who were not chosen as a representative sample. Care therefore needs to be taken in generalising the results beyond the original sample. However, where characteristics of the sample could be compared with other studies, as in the family structure of the children, the characteristics of the perpetrators, or the proportion of substantiated cases, there were more similarities than differences. Our findings that most registered children and their families received monitoring and limited practical help, rather than specific services aimed at compensating for the effects of maltreatment are also in line with those of other researchers (Gough et al., 1987; Corby, 1987).

A further limitation arises from the use of records as data sources. Investigations were not recorded in standard ways and some facts that might have seemed essential parts of any assessment (such as the families' material circumstances, racial background, child rearing practices and methods of discipline) were often missing. The quality of the data means that findings must be interpreted cautiously. The associations that we have found between certain characteristics of children and families and register status are presented tentatively but could be tested in further research. If methods of record keeping could be refined, and more standard methods of investigation and assessment be introduced, social services records would become a valuable source of data and monitoring would then be a more powerful research tool.

The child protection system as it exists in this country is unusual by international standards. In the USA, although reporting is mandatory, there is no comparable structure promoting inter-agency co-ordination. Elsewhere in Northern Europe, there is more reliance on voluntary, confidential and therapeutic responses (Christopherson, 1989). The English and Welsh system has grown up over the last two decades, driven by public scandals and enquiries which have always been able to point, retrospectively, to failure in co-ordination in individual cases (Noyes, 1991). There may have been just as many failures in inter-agency working in 'successful' cases: it may be fallacious to assume a causal relationship. However, much would be lost – in the development of joint policies at local level, identifying children at risk of significant harm and providing specialised services – if the thrust to maintain inter-agency cooperation were lost.

The new approach to children's services embodied in the Children Act 1989 provides an incentive for reconsidering the place of child protection procedures within provision for children and families. The Act places a general duty on local authorities to safeguard and promote the welfare of children in need through the provision of a range of family support services. A broad definition of 'need' is provided in Section 17, which would include most of the families in the present study. Section 47 places a duty on the local authority to investigate any case where it is suspected that a child is suffering significant harm or is likely to do so. This duty, supported by the guidance in *Working Together* (para 5), may be interpreted in such a way as to cut off all possibilities of responding to referrals expressing concern about a child's welfare *other* than by instituting investigation within a child protection framework. For example, the Manual of Procedures in one of the sample authorities stated:

Any allegation (actual or possible) of child abuse <u>or expression of concern regarding the welfare</u> *and safety of a child must be treated as a referral and preliminary investigations implemented . . . The Notification of Suspected Child Abuse Form must be completed on all referrals . . . (Our emphasis).*

However, such a rigid response may not be the intention of the legislation and supporting guidance. An 'expression of concern' about a child's welfare should not necessarily be treated in the same way as a definite suspicion that a child is at risk of suffering significant harm. Concerns about poor parental care, or about parent-adolescent disputes, or about a child's inappropriate behaviour at school – all of which were investigated under child protection procedures – might just as plausibly be interpreted as potential impairments of children's development, where support could be offered under section 17 of the Children Act. One 'low-rate' sample authority, for example, included in its Manual of Procedures a list of specific circumstances under which agencies should refer for a child protection investigation and stressed the need for clear, unambiguous referrals made, if necessary, only after consultation with advisers. This policy allows for the consideration of alternative approaches to families.

The Threshold for Child Protection Investigations

The child protection system deals with some children in great danger. Even this small monitoring exercise uncovered six children who died. However, large numbers of children who did not need protective intervention were being drawn into the system. If the ratio found in this study of six to seven investigations for every child placed on the register were duplicated nationally, it would mean that at least 180,000 investigations were taking place each year. In this study, about three-quarters of the children and families drawn into the child protection system received no protective intervention. Their being assessed as 'in need of protection', rather than as 'in need', probably accounted for the fact that a high proportion received no services at all as a result of their referral. Investigation showed there was no need for an inter-agency protection plan and other needs were not discussed although, as indicated by material stresses and family circumstances, they were often considerable. Too many families struggling with child rearing problems who came to the attention of social services departments were prematurely defined as potential child protection cases, rather than as families containing children in need.

Could more children and families be diverted from entry to the child protection system in the first place? Specific diversionary measures might be considered such as:

- Allowing more discretion in the treatment of referrals, so that an investigation for possible abuse is not an immediate or automatic response; or providing clearer guidance to all agencies as to the specific circumstances in which referrals for investigation should be made.

- Filtering out a higher proportion of referrals *after* checking reported concerns with other community agencies but *without* undertaking any investigative interviews.

- Introducing a 'severity' criterion which would exclude, for example, cases of 'excessive' discipline, slight injuries or allegation of sexual abuse supported by behaviour changes only.

- Introducing a 'substantiation' criterion – Certain types of allegation are rarely substantiated. On actuarial principles they might not be pursued, or be routinely dealt with under 'in need' procedures.

- Cases of neglect and emotional abuse are more likely to disappear from the child protection system without any services being offered. A more appropriate service might be offered if cases of neglect and emotional abuse were *first* assessed as 'children in need'. Only very serious cases where 'in need' procedures were proved to be inadequate would be referred for child protection investigations.

The Standard of Investigation

If there were a smaller number of investigations it would be possible for more of them to meet the standards of the best. Social workers carrying out child protection investigations perhaps need to be trained specialists, as police officers increasingly are, and some authorities have already moved in this direction. In any case, suspected cases should always be allocated to a named social worker. Recording of child protection investigations might be improved by developing standardised Investigation Report Forms, as was happening in some authorities, that would ensure all relevant factors have been included in the assessment. The Forms might include a formal Risk Assessment Summary, counter-signed by the manager or supervisor as well as the social worker. It should always be clearly stated whether the investigation substantiated the child protection concerns or not. Reasons should be given if the case is closed with no offer of services.

Case Conference Minutes

Minutes of initial protection conferences were usually lengthy documents, often summarising individual contributions. However, few contained a formal statement of the unresolved child protection issues that made an inter-agency plan necessary. These had to be inferred from the opinions expressed and sometimes from the chair's summary. The minutes usually listed the elements of the child protection plan but it was often unclear how the plan related to the supposed risks. The format of the minutes might be altered so that all elements of the child protection plan have to be explicitly related to the assessed risks. The desired outcomes could also be stated in the protection plan with some indication of time scales. This type of format might be more useful as a basis for the child protection review.

Removing Children's Names from the Register more Rapidly

The practice of some of the authorities in the present study showed that about a third of children's names could be removed from the register within six months *if* inter-agency child protection reviews were always held within six months of registration – as they were not in some of the sample authorities. There needed to be a structured format which enforced assessment of the continuing risk to the child. Retention of the child's name on the register needed to be explicitly justified, taking into account the continuing risk and whether there were objectives still to be achieved.

Post-Conference Services

It was discouraging to find that the better practice which appeared to exist in some authorities was not reflected in clear differences in children's outcomes. Research has already shown how difficult it is to achieve changes in 'abusive' families (Gough et al., 1988) but good practice was demonstrated in a number of authorities in the present study, notably in work with 'poor prognosis' young children who were separated from parents. The new provisions of the Children Act in respect of parental responsibility and the use of residence and contact orders were already being used imaginatively to increase the security of such children without severing family links. However, the conscientious monitoring of children at home (supplemented with practical help) which was the standard form of service, did not seem to get to grips with the forces that produced maltreatment, nor compensate for its effect on the child.

Efforts to improve inter-agency co-ordination have so far focussed very much on the early stages: the identification, investigation and labelling (through registration) of children needing protection. But co-ordination and cooperation are needed just as much at the treatment stage: education and health authorities largely control the specialist resources that might make a difference to child development. The emphasis of child protection policy might now shift towards the development and evaluation of more effective post-conference services within an inter-agency framework.

References

Association of Directors of Social Services (1981) *Child Abuse: Central Register Systems – The Level of Enquiries.* ADSS

Baldwin, N. and Spencer, N. (1993) Deprivation and child abuse: implications for strategic planning in children's services. *Children & Society* 7, 357–375

Besharov, D. J. (1985) Doing something about child abuse: the need to narrow the grounds for state intervention. *Harvard J. Law & Public Policy* 8(3) 539–559

Besharov, D. J. (1991) Child Abuse Reporting and Investigation: Policy Guidelines for Decision-Making. In Robin, M. ed. *Assessing Child Maltreatment Reports.* New York: Haworth Press

British Association of Social Workers (1978) *The Central Child Abuse Register.* Birmingham: BASW

Cann, A. J. (1989) The indefinition of child abuse. *Child Abuse Review* 3, 2, 27–30

Christopherson, J. (1989) European Child-Abuse Management Systems. In Stevenson, O. ed. *Child Abuse: Public Policy and Professional Practice.* Hemel Hempstead: Harvester

Clyde, The Lord (1992) *Report of the Inquiry into the Removal of Children from Orkney in February 1991.* London: HMSO House of Commons Papers 195

Corby, B. & Mills, C. (1986) Child abuse: risks and resources. *British Journal of Social Work* 16, 531–542

Corby, B. (1987) *Working With Child Abuse.* Milton Keynes: Open University Press

Creighton, S. J. & Noyes, P. (1989) *Child Abuse Trends in England and Wales 1983–1987.* London: NSPCC

Creighton, S. J. (1992) *Child Abuse Trends in England and Wales 1988–1990 and an Overview from 1973–1990.* London: NSPCC

DHSS (1974) *Memorandum on Non-Accidental Injury to Children.* LASSL (74) 13

DHSS (1976) *Non-Accidental Injury to Children.* LASSI (76) 2

DHSS (1980) *Child Abuse: Central Register Systems*. LASSL (80) 4: HN (80) 20

DHSS (1988) *Working Together: a guide to arrangements for inter-agency co-operation for the protection of children from abuse*. London: HMSO

Department of Health (1989–1993) *Surveys of Children and Young Persons on Child Protection Registers*. London: Department of Health

Department of Health (1988) *Protecting Children: a guide for social workers undertaking a comprehensive assessment*. London: HMSO

Department of Health Social Services Inspectorate (1990) *Report of an Inspection of Collaborative Working Arrangements Between Child Protection Agencies in Cleveland*. Gateshead: SSI Northern Region

Dingwall, J., Eekelaar, J. & Murray, T. (1983) *The Protection of Children: State Intervention and Family Life*. London: Tavistock

Famularo, R., Kinscherff, R. and Fenton, T. (1992) Parental substance abuse and the nature of child maltreatment. *Child Abuse & Neglect*. 16, 475–483

Family Rights Group (1986) *FRG's Response to the DHSS Consultation Paper Child Abuse: Working Together*. London: Family Rights Group

Finkelhor, D. (1979) *Sexually Victimised Children*. New York: Free Press

Geach, H. and Szwed. E. (1983) *Providing Civil Justice for Children*. London: Edward Arnold

Gibbons, J., Thorpe, S. & Wilkinson, P. (1990) *Family Support and Prevention: Studies in local areas*. London: HMSO

Giovannoni, J. (1989) Substantiated and unsubstantiated reports of child abuse and neglect. *Children & Youth Services Review* 11, 299–318

Gough, D. A., Boddy, F. A., Dunning, N. & Stone, F. H. (1987) *A Longitudinal Study of Child Abuse in Glasgow*. University of Glasgow & Greater Glasgow Health Board: Social Paediatric & Obstetric Research Unit.

Gough, D. A., Taylor, J. & Boddy, F. (1988) *Child Abuse Intervention: A Review of the Literature*. University of Glasgow.

Hallett, C. and Stevenson, O. (1980) *Child Abuse: Aspects of Inter-Professional Co-Operation*. London: Allen & Unwin

Home Office, Department of Health, Department of Education & Science & Welsh Office (1991) *Working Together Under the Children Act 1989*. London: HMSO

Jones, J., George, E., Goldsmith, L., Hussell, C. & Llewellyn, G. (1986) *Child Abuse: Policy, Practice and Procedures*. London: Borough of Westminster

Little, M. and Gibbons, J. (1993) Predicting the rate of children on the child protection register. *Research, Policy & Planning*, 10, 15–17

Magura, S. et al., (1987) *Assessing Risk and Measuring Change in Families: the Family Risk Assessment Scales*. Washington DC: Child Welfare League

Meddin, B. J. (1985) Assessment of risk in child abuse and neglect case investigation. *Child Abuse & Neglect*, 9, 57–62

Noyes, P. (1991) *Child Abuse: A Study of Inquiry Reports*. London: HMSO

Parton, N. (1985) *The Politics of Child Abuse*. London: Macmillan

Pecora, P. J. (1991) Investigating Allegations of Child Maltreatment: Strengths and limitations of current risk-assessment systems. In Robin, M. ed., *op. cit.*

Robin, M. (1991) *Assessing Child Maltreatment Reports*. New York: Haworth Press

Royal Belfast Hospital and Queens University (1990) *Child Sexual Abuse in Northern Ireland*. Antrum: Greystone

Starr, R. H. ed. (1981) *Child Abuse Prediction: Policy Implications*. Cambridge, Mass.: Ballinger

Tilley, N. and Burke, R. (1988) Acting rationally: child abuse registrations. *Community Care* 8/12, 16–17

Waterhouse, L. and Carnie, J. (1992) Assessing child protection risk. *British Journal of Social Work* 22, 47–60

Name Index

Complementary studies also available from HMSO Books include:

Parental Perspectives in Cases of Suspected Child Abuse
Hedy Cleaver and Pam Freeman (The Dartington Team)
HMSO 1995. ISBN 0 11 321786 2

Child Protection Practice: Private Risks and Public Remedies
Elaine Farmer and Morag Owen (The University of Bristol Team)
HMSO 1995. ISBN 0 11 321787 0

The Prevalence of Child Sexual Abuse in Britain
Deborah Ghate and Liz Spencer (Social and Community Planning Research)
HMSO 1995. ISBN 0 11 321783 8

Development After Physical Abuse in Early Childhood: A Follow-Up Study of Children on Protection Registers
Jane Gibbons, Bernard Gallagher, Caroline Bell and David Gordon (University of East Anglia)
HMSO 1995. ISBN 0 11 321790 0

Inter-agency Coordination and Child Protection
Christine Hallett (The University of Stirling)
HMSO 1995. ISBN 0 11 321789 7

Working Together in Child Protection
Elizabeth Birchall (The University of Stirling)
HMSO 1995. ISBN 0 11 321830 3

Paternalism or Partnership? Family Involvement in the Child Protection Process
June Thoburn, Ann Lewis and David Shemmings (University of East Anglia)
HMSO 1995. ISBN 0 11 321788 9

Messages from Research
HMSO 1995. ISBN 0 11 321781 1

Printed in the United Kingdom for HMSO
Dd301475 11/95 C10 G3397 10170